T0193233

YES!
JESUS
IS THE ONLY WAY TO
HEAVEN

YES!
JESUS
IS THE ONLY WAY TO
HEAVEN

Thomas saith unto him, Lord, we know not whither thou goest; and how can we know the way? Jesus saith unto him, **I am the way, the truth, and the life: no man cometh unto the Father, but by me.** John 14:5-6

From the Testimony of a Traveler Now Heaven Bound

RENEE E. WOODS

iUniverse

YES! JESUS IS THE ONLY WAY TO HEAVEN
FROM THE TESTIMONY OF A TRAVELER NOW HEAVEN BOUND

iUniverse books may be ordered through booksellers or by contacting:

iUniverse
1663 Liberty Drive
Bloomington, IN 47403
www.iuniverse.com
1-800-Authors (1-800-288-4677)

Because of the dynamic nature of the Internet, any web addresses or links contained in this book may have changed since publication and may no longer be valid. The views expressed in this work are solely those of the author and do not necessarily reflect the views of the publisher, and the publisher hereby disclaims any responsibility for them.

Any people depicted in stock imagery provided by Getty Images are models, and such images are being used for illustrative purposes only.
Certain stock imagery © Getty Images.

Scripture quotations from the Holy Bible, King James Version (Authorized Version).
First published in 1611. Quoted from the KJV Classic Reference Bible.

ISBN: 978-1-5320-8428-7 (sc)
ISBN: 978-1-5320-8427-0 (e)

Library of Congress Control Number: 2019914800

Print information available on the last page.

iUniverse rev. date: 12/10/2019

CONTENTS

dedicate this inspirational book to my Father, the one and only (*true and living*) God, to Jesus my Lord and Savior (*my way maker*), and to the Holy Spirit (*my Helper*), and to all the witnesses of my life journey, including the transition into the family of God. Thank you all for encouraging me along the way, to my wonderful husband, who has supported and prayed with me through all of life's joyful days and times of adversities and growing pains. You have and still stand with me as I proceed forward to achieve God's assignment for my life. I just have to say that, prior to our engagement, the first time I met you, I pronounced that one day you would be my husband, and this was a strong heart-felt feeling that I had. Thank you, Dear, for the pillows you have placed behind my back while I was typing and picking them up when they fell on the floor and for lifting me up out of the bed when I was in so much pain after sitting for a long while. I love you, my dear. To my daughter, thank you for all your love and support. I thank God that he gave me a chance to see you grow into an awesome woman of God and a great mother, and to my three Granddaughters, who encouraged me continuously to complete this book. My dear Mother, who read over the beginning part of my unfinished manuscript—in 2016 she went home to be with the Lord. She was very supportive to building up the kingdom of God. Mom always used her gifts of singing and playing the piano to the glory of God. Also, my sister, who was one of few words but would always take time to listen to me speak about the goodness of God in my life. Thank you, Jesus, for saving her; she went home to be with the Lord in 2015. Everyone needs a *BFF (best friends forever);* to my dear friend, who has never changed on me, you are a loving, awesome, caring person, who has always been there for me; you are like no other—a true sister in the Lord. Thank you for not calling me that much when I was attempting to accomplish this assignment! I appreciate all the encouraging words and consistent prayers that I know you sent up for me. You are a treasure; thank you. God Bless all of you!

FOREWORD INTRODUCTION

reetings and blessings, Dr. and Pastor Renee Woods has written a profound book that will stir the heart of the reader! It will cause you to think about your journey and all that you have been through in life to get you past where you are today. This book *"Yes! Jesus is the Only Way!"* is a profound book that will cause the reader to examine their belief system, their life, and all the religions in the world to come to one conclusion: that Jesus Christ is who he said he is in the bible—The way, the truth, and the life! (John 14:6)

This book is full of testimonies and scriptures that will cause the reader to think about life, death, burial, and resurrection of Jesus Christ, as there is no other like Him in all the earth. The testimonies of a traveler will inspire you and give you clarity in this earthly journey called life, in God which God himself has placed us!

Read it with an open mind, as I am sure there will be many opinions of some sort. Nevertheless, for those of us who have experienced the transforming *power of Jesus Christ in this earthly journey, we can truly say that, "Yes! Jesus is the only way!" May God bless you and smile upon you as you read this book by an anointed vessel of God whom I consider a good friend, spiritual daughter, and fellow laborer in Christ!*

Jamal E. Quinn, Senior Pastor

Firm Foundation Christian Fellowship

Riverview, FL

INTRODUCTION

There are several kinds of travelers in the world today; have you considered which one you are? Here are a few examples for you to examine and embrace. The **first traveler**, who has taken time to plan and organize themselves, is called the **prepared traveler**. The **second traveler** is a **spontaneous trip taker**, motivated by inner impulses, unplanned actions. The **third traveler** is the *911* **emergency must go individual!** At any cost, cheap tickets are not available currently— only high-priced ones—but that would not be an issue for this traveler at all. It is most important for him or her to reach their destination A.S.A.P.

Have you ever seen someone who is at the airport and getting ready to board their flight, but this person seems to be confused about where he is? Something is definitely wrong. What has happened to this traveler? His behavior is of one who seems to be *lost and wandering. This person is out of touch with reality.* In this crowded and very busy airport, people are staring at this wonder. They do not understand the behavior, this is traveler **number four**.

The **fifth** and final traveler is one who is *financially secure* in life, living large, and having an extravagant lavish lifestyle. Their *modus operandi* is flamboyant—able to take a vacation at any time, as money is never a problem for them—traveling by limousine, expensive automobiles, private jets and boats—traveling anywhere on this planet.

I hope and pray that the readers of this book will see through the testimony of a traveler, whose destination would have been in a place called hell!—where there would be no escape. Thank God, that trip has been forever canceled! I have been re-routed, and one day I will enter into a place called heaven. This destination comes with everlasting benefits.

The Holy writ *(Bible)* to a Christian traveler, *per se*, is a spiritual navigation system *(Catechism)*—a summary of principles for the practice of religion. As partakers of the truth, we become equipped to live a life which is predicated on faith in God. The Bible is sealed with the manufacturer's guarantee—a road map consisting of Illustrations, pictorials, and profound analogies—everything one would need to guide them through life's journey. **All scripture is given by inspiration of God and is profitable for doctrine, for reproof, for correction, for instruction in righteousness *(2 Timothy 3:16)*.**

In today's society, people use many different forms of transportation. We have cars, boats Planes, trains, buses etc. A traveler, whose mode of transportation is a motor vehicle and being the Operator, must always pay close attention to their surroundings. They are to be focused always, keeping their eyes on the road *(no texting)*—avoid distractions; be a defensive driver. When traveling, safety is very important; it can be life altering. A person must always watch out for suspicious characters; danger is always lurking in some form or fashion—wild drivers who can be under the influence and have become a dangerous weapon behind the wheel of a car.

A stranger can bring harm, and dangerous situations can develop. You also can be car jacked. Don't ever open your doors for just anybody to become a passenger in your life. One must heed the warning signs and always drive with caution. In other words, travelers, the enemy has you on his mind. He is a thief **(John 10:10)**; he is wandering around looking for drivers who are unprepared for their journey **(that's one without Christ)**.

A child of God is a Christian who is on a journey traveling through this life on earth, adhering daily to divine instructions—the word of God. A student is one who carefully studies their road map, following it successfully, and obeying the warning signs also.

Study to shew thyself approved unto God, a workman that needeth not to be ashamed, rightly dividing the word of truth. (2Timothy 2:15)

When one becomes disciplined from obeying and following God's instructions **(The Holy Bible)** Daily, being guided by the Holy Spirit, this traveler is empowered and fully equipped for service in the kingdom of God. They are determined, productive, and focused only on their Father's business—a life that truly manifests real biblical truths via "faith in action". **(James 2: 17)**

Thus also **faith by itself, if it does not have works, is dead.**

By activating one's faith in God and proceeding in His divine will for your life makes the journey bright and fulfilling—never a dull moment.

All of creation has a starting point and a beginning, the birth canal of a mother's womb, which is a prepared place for the new traveler in their appointed time, proceeding from one place to another into this God-created homestead called earth. It's appointed for man to die, but one can receive the promise of eternal life (a gift), only available by receiving the Gospel of the Kingdom of God through Jesus Christ. There are people in this society who are truly seeking an answer to this prolific question: What must I do to inherit eternal life (Heaven)? Some are trying to understand and find answers that would validate the very existence of a heavenly kingdom by using human reasoning.

These five questions are similar in human reasoning:

> *(1).* What will happen when one takes their last breath on this earth?
>
> *(2).* When one dies, is the grave their destination?
>
> *(3).* Is there life after death / eternity?
>
> *(4).* Are Christians the only ones who can go to heaven?
>
> *(5).* Is Jesus the only way to heaven?

Let's travel on! Could it be that one of these questions is yours?

The answer you are diligently seeking has already been revealed and is only available to those who are ready and serious about receiving the truth that Jesus Christ is the only way to the Father (God) in His heavenly kingdom! It is a must for all to take a self-examination today, right at this very moment. Are you sure that you are on the right track or **pathway**? So please keep traveling by reading on; this is your map to guide you on your way to get the most important answer to your question! If you are already on this only pathway to God, you can share with your friends, family, and others who are seeking the truth.

Poem: ***SEEKERS***

I am seeking to find my way, in this dark and dreary world in which I stay.

Looking here and searching there, perception is sometimes so unclear, maybe it's just fear.

Critical times have made me blind, I feel like I'm losing my mind.

Paid a hefty price for a disobedient life, it has only lead to heartaches and strife.

So much shame and blame I claim, what became a horrible game to play.

Seeking a way out, but in time I find more troubles along the line.

My pride is on the rise, bringing tears to my eyes, like a river streaming down my face.

Much disgrace, but I still run this race with agonizing pain that I sustained.

Someone has played a horrible, deadly game; consumed with shame— have I been framed?

Only I am to blame; I played the devil's game, for my shame brought me no gain.

Dreams have faded away, visions were no longer displayed, but thank God it's a new day, so I pray. This seeker has found a brighter day that made a way out of no way!

I prayed for help from the only light that shines so bright and dispel the darkness of my life.

I knock, and the door opens. Serving the Lord with all my might, tasting his word is such a delight.

No longer a seeker, for I have been found and will get a crown.

Ask, and it shall be given you; seek, and ye shall find; knock, and it shall be opened unto you: For everyone that asketh receiveth; and he that seeketh findeth; and to him that knocketh it shall be opened. (Matthew 7:7-8)

CHAPTER 1

God! Creator of all things

The Bible is the authentic word of God, written by Holy men who were divinely inspired by the Holy Spirit. The Old Testament and New Testament Christian Bible contains 66 books. The Bible is a masterpiece of spiritual inspiration given by God almighty, the creator of all things! No man without divine guidance has done this great work.

For the prophecy came not in old time by the will of man: but holy men of God spake as they were moved by the Holy Ghost. (2 Peter 1:21)

Holy men of God had the privilege to pen such profound biblical literature that reveals God's plan for the redemption of humanity. The very existence of God is revealed in nature and the Holy writ, this unequivocal fact, in the beginning—God! This very first statement gives credence to the creator and ruler of His universe, which man has

1

been privileged to occupy. God is a Supreme Being. Perfect in power, wisdom, and full of goodness, the LORD reigns. **The LORD reigneth; let the people tremble: he sitteth between the cherubims; let the earth be moved. The LORD is great in Zion; and he is high above all the people. (Psalm 99:1-2)**

He is *"omnipotent"*, which means God is all powerful, **(almighty)** unlimited, infinite, and the creator of all things ("yes he is"). **And I heard as it were the voice of a great multitude, and as the voice of many waters, and as the voice of mighty thunderings, saying,**

Alleluia: for the Lord God omnipotent reigneth. (Revelation 19:6)

God is omnipresent. He is an all-present, everywhere God **(omnipresent)**. In the Old Testament Book of **Isaiah (Chapter 66:1)**, we find these words: **Thus, saith the LORD, the heaven is my throne, and the earth is my footstool: where is the house that ye build unto me? And where is the place of my rest?**

God is a Spirit; his "dwelling place is in heaven". **(1King 8:30) And hearken thou to the supplication of thy servant, and of thy people Israel, when they shall pray toward this place: and hear thou in heaven thy dwelling place: and when thou hearest, forgive.** The last chapter of the Holy Bible describes God as, **"I am Alpha and Omega, the beginning and the end, the first and the last. (Rev. 22:13)**

For the born-again believer (Christians), the primacy of God is reassuring—the importance of knowing that your heavenly father is in control; nothing gets past Him. When I was without redemption, I was spiritually dead, dead and blind, unaware of this divine revelation of knowing that God knew everything about me and what I was up to—be it good or bad choices. Those who make many good or bad decisions in life, there must be an understanding that you are being watched daily, "under surveillance and recorded".

(Proverbs 15:3) The eyes of the LORD are everywhere, keeping watch on the wicked and the good. (Job 34:21) His eyes are on the ways of men; he sees their every step.

In the story of the fall of man in the Garden of Eden, Adam and Eve, after they sinned against God, heard His voice, speaking unto Adam. God was walking in the garden in the cool of the day **(Genesis 3:8).** Their first response was to hide from the very presence of their creator, behind the tree in the garden that God created. For sin caused a ripple effect in their lives; their eyes were opened, and they perceived that they were naked; being in this state was once the norm. They never knew these feelings of shame before.

They were always in the garden with nothing on psychically, so the very embarrassment of disobedience to their creator God causes them to behave in an unfamiliar manner. I like to say they were playing hide and go seek, but they could not hide what they did or where they were from God. We see them operating as seamstresses, creating something to cover themselves up, sewing together the very fig leaves that their creator made. They invented the very first aprons, per-se. **(Genesis 3:7)** And the eyes of them both were opened, and they knew that they were naked; and they sewed fig leaves together and made themselves aprons.

A very important fact for all mankind to understand is that no one can hide from Almighty God our creator. **(Isaiah 40:28) Hast thou not known? Hast thou not heard, that the everlasting God, the LORD,**

the Creator of the ends of the earth, fainteth not, neither is weary? There is no searching of his understanding.

God knows all about you. He created your very existence here on earth, and he is with his children during difficult circumstances and traumatic times. Even when you don't want anyone to know what you have endured, God knows. Don't lie to yourself. Even when you are dealing with the situation, you need a permanent fix **(help)**. It is mankind's responsibility to stop hiding from the creator. We must recognize that there is no handling life's circumstances without Him.

Adam and Eve needed the love and mercy of their Father in a tangible way. God moved by preparing them for what they would face—earthly elements in which they must have on the proper attire—by covering His Children physically and spiritually. God made clothing for them. What was wrong with the outfit they made from the fig leaves? The fig leaves design would not sustain them, the leaves being removed from the tree and its roots supply. God sacrificed an animal to cover their sin, for God declared the payment for mankind' sin is death; blood must be shed to cover sin.

(Leviticus 17:11) For the life of the flesh is in the blood: and I have given it to you upon the altar to make an atonement for your souls: for it is the blood that maketh atonement for the soul. (Hebrews 9:22) And almost all things are by the law purged with blood: and without shedding of blood is no remission.

Creator of all humanity and every living thing, all creation began with God—His great masterpiece embellished with the paintbrush of his powerful vocal expression. His spoken word that resounded throughout the darkness and through the emptiness of an unformed environment, speaking the universe into existence.

(Genesis 1:3) Then God said, "Let there be light"; and there was light.

And, Thou, Lord, in the beginning hast laid the foundation of the earth; and the heavens are the works of thine hands: *(Hebrews 1:10)*

In our society, where we have freedom of religion, there are some religious groups that oppose Christian doctrinal truths. Some have even insisted they are talking about the same God that we believe in, yet they call him by different names. In the canonized Holy Bible, there's no other deity—only Almighty God! There isn't any mention of evolution, nor is there any credence given to Darwin's theory. Our God isn't the product of a scientific method or manmade graven image. He is eternal, the beginning, and the end. *"In the beginning was God"*! *(Genesis 1:1)*

(Romans 1:20) **For the invisible things of him from the creation of the world are clearly seen, being understood by the things that are made, even his eternal power and Godhead; so that they are without excuse.**

When I think about God, at the beginning of all things existing, it's with amazement and assurance to know that there is only one God! This statement is fact. I speak from the personal experience of having encountered the false gods of this world in many forms, be it an object or physical or material image worshipped by mankind, making them an idol, forsaking the one and only living God, putting Him on the "back burner", instead of embracing His agape love ("supra-natural") and abiding in the presences of the Lord through a cultivated relationship with Him. The false sources have become an idol in many forms, such as ungodly substances, addictive behaviors, drugs, alcohol, sex, and love of money, controlling and sucking the life out of people.

(2 Corinthians 4:4) In whom the god of this world hath blinded the minds of them which believe not, lest the light of the glorious gospel of Christ, who is the image of God, should shine unto them.

(1 Corinthians 8:4) . . . **we know that an idol is nothing in the world, and that there is no other God but one.**

He is the master of us all! Don't be confused about his ownership, for his seal was placed on mankind when He formed man in His own image ("Satisfaction guaranteed"). If his property is broken or damaged, causing malfunctions, you can always go back to manufacturer. Ownership on the earthy planet can be seen from looking at a person whose occupation is a business person—who is the sole owner of many corporations. He alone is the boss, the founder of what he started. God, who is the master potter, ...formed man of the dust of the ground, and breathed into his nostrils the breath of life; and man became a living soul. *(Genesis 2:7)* God said it was not good for man *(Adam)* to be alone, for all creation in the Garden of Eden had a mate. God's first operation in the garden took place, and woman *(Eve)* was given to Adam. **(Genesis 2:18)** God gave them their very first home, and they resided in a place called the Garden of Eden. Adam and Eve were given dominion over the earth, along with the privilege to take care of God's garden *(Genesis 2:15)*.

When God completed His masterpiece creation, He said, "It is very good." This statement validates the authenticity of His ownership. When I was a child, I was taught that God is real and that He loves me.

My mother would break out singing gospel hymns, such as "Jesus loves me this I know, for the Bible tells me so!" I remember hearing many gospel songs sung at home. The gift of music runs in my family, for my mother played the piano. My two brothers also are musically and vocally inclined. Two of my other siblings and I just make a joyful noise! My mother, along with her siblings, sang in a group called "Gospel Singers." Two of my favorite hymns that I heard sung at home were *He's got the whole world in His hands* and *How Great Thou Art.* These songs are wonderful hymns, and to me they were seeds of the word of God that were planted in my heart—that God is the creator of all things, and he is great and mighty. As a family, we were instructed to pray to God daily, and we were not strangers in attending church.

Now that I have a personal, intimate relationship with the Lord, and I am aware of His unconditional love for me, I have committed and dedicated my life to Him. As a young believer and child of God, I thought that being a child of God would be a bed of roses, but the road of ease was a misnomer. I quickly found out that it was not so. I matured quickly and developed tough skin as a believer. As I reflect upon my life as a new Christian, I recall having a discussion with my husband about joining one of the ministries in the organization we attended. He gave me a pep talk, and it went like this, "Everybody isn't going to love you." I looked up at him with my eyes sticking out of my head in a state of shock. It was hard for me to believe that! Well, I joined a group, and on the day of rehearsal, a controversial conversation occurred about my response to a question of choosing a uniform attire color. What colors would we like to wear on Sunday? With my happy self and full of joy, I raised my hand and said,

"Yellow and black would be nice," —two of my favorite colors. Suddenly, one of the members rudely interjected: "I don't have money to be buying those colors." Her tone was unkind, sharp, and insensitive. She wasn't acting like a Christian to me at that moment. This might not have meant anything to someone else, but to me it was not a representation of God's love, especially to me as a new believer in Christ. If I did not know Gods' presence in my life, I would have run out of that church and never returned, since I was a very sensitive person in that time of my infancy as a new believer in the body of Christ.

I quickly recalled what my husband had said. He was speaking from experience of dealing with those who are in the church and sometimes don't act like the church. Learning how to deal with those who say one thing and live another was challenging at that time. I had to learn what the bible says about the behavior of others and how I was to exemplify Christ. In other words, what would Jesus do? Well, in my search through the scriptures, I came upon a story about a good tree and what kind of fruit it bears ("good fruit"), for we who are Christian are depicted as a tree with branches that fruit grow on. There are good trees which produce only good fruit and bad (or evil) trees with fruit that's corrupt. *(Matthew 7: 18-20)* Fruits that come from a good tree manifest the fruit of the Spirit: *(Galatian 5:22-23)* "wherefore by their fruits we will know them."

When I pondered on this metaphor, my heart went out for those who were in the church holding offices but living contrary to the word of God and not being dealt with and removed them from their position, for sin must be addressed. Jesus died to cleanse us from all sin. God's people must be Holy as He is holy. I remember entering the house of prayer, and I smelled alcohol reeking from a person who was in a leadership position. As a new believer, this was totally shocking to me, but I did not let that stop me from coming to worship. I learned how to stay focused and on course in my personal relationship with God, understanding that my destiny is ordained by God, having purpose and determined not to let anyone or myself get me off track.

I make note that those persons were in a good place to get their breakthrough: a spiritual hospital. Due to the sin in the camp, my Christian walk could have been hindered. As a new Christian, it was hurtful to see others in the church that were not serious about their walk with God. I was so hurt that I shed a few tears when the choir incident occurred. My husband reminded me that he warned me. However, the word of God kept me, and every time I reach back and touch my neck and feel the scar (I broke my neck in a car accident), I just remain content in Jesus, determined to continue my Christian journey, no matter what I have to go through. Knowing the realness of the love of God in my life kept me when I was rejected and abandoned by other believers. I knew that these experiences were part of the preparation— not for where I was but for where I was going. I found myself praising God and forever thankful that I was no longer on crack or addicted to drugs and alcohol.

Through my experiences, I understood that I was grafted into a new arena, which consisted of spiritual warfare. The ringleader was the devil, and he was trying hard to turn me back to a life of sin. I have heard some people say that the church has a lot of hypocrites. I pondered on this and came up with this: If all the people who felt that way left the church, who would see Jesus? For mankind cannot see Jesus. They can only see Him through the believers. Through us the reflection of Jesus is seen, for the Bible speaks *(The words of Jesus)* of two types of people in a parable: wheat *(Christian)* and the tares *(sinners)*.

(Matthew 13:24-30) **Another parable put he forth unto them, saying, The kingdom of heaven is likened unto a man which sowed**

good seed in his field; But while men slept, his enemy came and sowed tares among the wheat and went his way. But when the blade was sprung up, and brought forth fruit, then appeared the tares also. So, the servants of the householder came and said unto him, Sir, didst not thou sow good seed in thy field? From whence then hath it tares? He said, unto them, <u>an enemy hath done this</u>. The servants said unto him, Wilt thou then that we go and gather them up? But he said, Nay; lest while ye gather up the tares, ye root up also the wheat with them. Let both grow together until the harvest: and in the time of harvest I will say to the reapers, Gather ye together first the tares, and bind them in bundles to burn them: but gather the wheat into my barn.

There isn't a perfect church or Christian. It doesn't matter how long you have been in church or a believer. We all make mistakes and fall short. Thank God for His grace and mercy. God will never leave us nor forsake us. As we travel this road, our Christian journey will be one of challenges. We must remain confident that our God through the power of the Holy Spirit will help us navigate through it all. Let your conversation be without covetousness; and be content with such things as ye have: for he hath said, I will never leave thee, nor forsake thee. (*Hebrew 13:5*)

What I have truly learned through my growing pains is that God is always with me. His love never fails! His love is relentless! ***GOD is really my creator!*** His Word is true and will never return unto Him void. Perseverance is an essential part of my destiny-driven life, for in Him I live, move, and have my being. Truly trusting in God is a sure blessing! I am pressing towards the mark of the prize of the high calling which is in Christ Jesus. In hard times, retreating is not an option, for, as believing traveler, I know where I am headed, and God is in control of my destiny. In times of adversity, I must stand and realize that trials are producing spiritual growth and drawing me into a closer relationship with God. The trials cause me to lean and depend on God. He is my refuge and the strength of my life.

(Romans 5:3-5) And not only so, but we glory in tribulations also: knowing that tribulation worketh patience; And patience, experience; and experience, hope: And hope maketh not ashamed; because the love of God is shed abroad in our hearts by the Holy Ghost which is given unto us.

God's presence in my life is very powerful. I know that He is God, and besides Him there is no other. He is forever with me and lets me know that no matter what problems arise in my life, they will make me better and not bitter. God's love is expressed and evident by Him giving His only-begotten son, Jesus, as a living sacrifice for all mankind.

One night, about 2:00 a.m., I recall lying in bed trying to get a good night's sleep. I was meditating on the goodness of the Lord, how much He truly loved me, and how I was so grateful that He saved me from sin. As I was sobbing *(crying)* with tears flowing on my pillow, my husband heard me and asked if I was okay. I responded yes, I am alright. This heartfelt emotion was twofold: first, my tears flowed from my eyes for all mankind, concerned for their fate, and secondly, the pain of knowing the destination of those who did not have God in their life. I prayed earnestly for God's grace and mercy for them, that they would hear, believe, and receive the Gospel of Jesus Christ. I prayed that they would receive salvation and be set free from a life of sin.

On this night, I could not stop thinking about my born-again experience, experiencing Jesus Christ as my Lord and savior. At this stage in my new born-again life, all I knew was I was saved, no longer bound to a life of sin. I would compare my awakening experience to having new spiritual sight. When a newborn baby enters this world, their sight is blurry at birth. They must learn to see clearly over time as they grow up.

They must learn to focus their eyes and sharpen their visual abilities. As a babe in Christ, I knew so little at that time about God, but one thing I was sure about: that my life was once a natural disaster, in which devastation was readily seen. The people I once hung out with were very much in the same state of sin that I was in. My relationships with those whom I considered to be my friends consisted of recreational activities that displayed our dysfunctional behaviors as we indulged in drugs and alcohol. I truly wanted everybody I knew to receive salvation through Jesus. He is the only way out of a dead-end life. Only God the creator of all things has a plan for my life, and for sure He will complete it. One of my favorite Scriptures that always encourages me every time I read or meditate on it is *Philippians 1:6:* **Being confident of this very thing, that he which hath begun a good work in you will perform it until the day of Jesus Christ.**

CHAPTER 2

Man's Deviation from God

One of my most vivid childhood memories is a time when I was disobedient to one of the rules and regulations of my parents. We were told to ask first before taking anything from the refrigerator or cabinets. One day, I took a cookie from the cookie jar without permission.

My parents noticed that cookies were missing. They asked me and my siblings who the culprit was. No confessions from anyone of us, and I said nothing, for I was the one who stole the cookie from the cookie jar. My siblings were all chastised for one person's action. The consequences for my action of stealing caused a domino effect. We all got chastised for my disobedience.

When I read the stories of Adam and Eve in the Book of Genesis, it was very clear to me how man deviated from God: not obeying the

God-given directives of what they were to do and not do concerning the tree of good and evil. The Heavenly Father was providing and caring for His children, giving them everything that they had ever needed. Adam and Eve responded with an act of defiance to God and making excuses for what they had done. Now mankind is the recipient of their choice to disobey what they were told not to do by the Father.

In the Garden of Eden, God provided a home for Adam and Eve to live and have fellowship with Him. When they disobeyed the instructions of God, they deviated from the perfect plan that he designed for their lives with Him. Their acceptance of the deception of the devil, who came to Eve in the form of a talking serpent, caused them to be in a state of sin (spiritual death), which is separation from God. A new behavior is displayed by Adam and Eve toward their creator, who provided everything they needed in the Garden of Eden. Now, they are hiding from Him—God who sees all and knows all.

And they heard the voice of the LORD God walking in the garden in the cool of the day: and Adam and his wife hid themselves from the presence of the LORD God amongst the trees of the garden. (Genesis 3:8)

The Holy fellowship that they had with their heavenly Father had been severed. **But your iniquities have separated between you and your God, and your sin have hid his face from you, that he will not hear. (Isaiah 59:2)**

Sin brought about a spiral effect—a chain reaction throughout the life of man.

1 Corinthians 15:22 states, "For as in Adam all die, even so in Christ shall all be made alive." The bible says that as in Adam all die, so now all of humanity was born in sin and shapen in iniquity; the depraved condition of mankind is evident today.

It is interesting to note that they were created as free moral agents with the ability to choose right from wrong. Man, in his original state, was given the ability to be obedient and to make the right choices. The corruptor (the serpent) was prowling and attacked God's children to get them to disobey God. Yes, Eve yielded to temptation and gave to her husband, and Adam followed suit, taking the fruit and eating. Both disobeyed God; they both fell into sin losing their innocence. This rendered them naked and ashamed. Their disobedience brought about God's righteous judgment, resulting in spiritual separation from the very presence of God *(death)*.

(Genesis 2:16-17) **And the LORD God commanded the man, saying, "Of every tree of the garden you may freely eat: But of the tree of the knowledge of good and evil, thou shall not eat of it: for in the day that thou eatest thereof thou shalt surely die."**

God in His righteous judgment expelled them from the Garden of Eden. They had to seek a new home and dwelling place outside of the garden. They were the first man and woman on planet earth, and their disobedience altered the course of humanity.

SIN BREEDS SIN! (BAD TO WORSE)

When I think of mankind's fall in the Garden of Eden, the resulting sin, and its spiraling effect, it caused things to go from bad to worse, breeding more sin throughout time—from generation to generation.

Chaos was evident in the first family, leading to jealousy and murder, as Cain kills his brother Abel. The scripture says, **"And Cain talked with Abel his brother: and it came to pass, when they were in the field, that Cain rose up against Abel his brother, and slew him."** *(Genesis 4:8)*

Separation from God breeds a life of sin, and a heavenly antidote is indeed needed. A sin stain is like a plague that spreads. The acronym for sin is "spiritual insight needed"! The only stain remover that promised to make a way out for mankind was Jesus Christ. *(Genesis 3:15)* **"And I will put enmity between thee and the woman, and between thy seed and her seed: it shall bruise thy head, and thou shalt bruise his heel."** As a mother has the role of taking care of her family, I had many responsibilities. One of them was teaching and instructing my daughter what was right and wrong behavior.

Primary lessons consisted of moral standards that would guide her in the way that one must conduct themselves in right living. Back in those days, respect for the elderly was what you did (today, help us Lord), and respect for law enforcement people in general! I would explain to her the consequences of one's decisions and actions that would result in life, due to those decisions.

I was speaking from one who traveled the path of disobedience to my own parents, being rebellious as a youth and young adult. I was very hard-headed and full of myself, going from bad to worse. I was sin sick until I was redeemed by the blood of the Lamb. Then and only then was I able to share the answer for the only way out of sin that separates us from God.

We must understand there is always a culprit in the mist, working against us, who will use anyone to keep you bound in sin. This culprit is out to deceive, introducing mankind to worldly pleasures that breed sin.

(1 John 2:15-17) **"Love not the world, neither the things that are in the world. If any man loves the world, the love of the father is not in him. For all that is in the world, the lust of the flesh, and the lust of the eyes, and the pride of life, is not of the Father, but is of the world.**

And the world passes away, and the lust thereof: but he that doeth the will God abides forever." Have you ever purchased an item that you thought was genuine, but later you found out it was a copy, a knockoff, imitation, counterfeit, fake, or not the real thing? This is an example of how Satan works. He puts things in our lives that appear to be authentic, but it is not so. Some may have prior experience of meeting someone, and you may have even stated that yes! God gave this person to me! They appeared to be everything you hoped for in a person; they were packaged and wrapped so well (in other words, looking good, pleasant to the eye). But when the package is opened, it's not what you thought it would be *(That's Satan the deceiver,* whose daily job is to entice mankind to continue in a sinful life and stay in it).

Universal Sin: Transgression of God's Law *(1 John 3:4)* **Whosoever commits sin transgresses also the law, for sin is the transgression of the law.**

(Psalm 51:5) **Behold, I was shaped in iniquity; and in sin did my mother conceive me.**

When a person yields to the flesh and its lustful desires, the result is a perverted and ungodly lifestyle. The flesh will lead one into an unprofitable life with a dead end. Warning signs and godly direction will be dismissed by the "fleshy mindset." A roadblock of sin has been placed before the traveler, trying to keep them bound up in sinful acts that consume their life.

The ultimate purpose is to stop them from being reconciled to God. The plague of sin breeds more sin, spreading its poison, lies, deceit, and trickery. Sin deceives people every second, minute, and hour of the day. The devil has no problem using his helpers to work overtime to destroy the life of a person who is driven by lusts, passions of the flesh, and the pride of life. The enemy has no preferences. He wants everyone to be entangled in sin. He tries daily to make sin enticing and attractive. When people choose not to be connected to God by accepting Jesus into their life, they are vulnerable to the evil forces of Satan. He sabotages their destiny, and they reap the consequences of destruction.

This world is filled with counterfeit gods that some people choose to worship, and in doing so this pathway leads people straight to hell. **Proverbs 14:12 says there is a way that seems right to a man but its end is the way to death.**

All of humanity was born and shapen in iniquity, we all started off in this world in a state of sin, blinded to the very truth that would set us free. It's not just the sinful acts which we do, but we inherited it from the first man and woman:

Adam and Eve, the parents of humanity, from whom we derived our sin nature.

Mankind, whom God loves so very much, needed a way of escape. Deliverance was a needed thing. Jesus came into the world to take away our sin nature and give us a new nature. Through His Blood, our sins are washed away, and we are made a new creation. It is the blood that Jesus shed at Calvary on a tree in the shape of a cross, the suffering Lamb of God. The Messiah, redeemer, frees us from our sin state as we surrender all to him, **"repentance is our door knob" per se**. Out with the old, and in with the new. He prepares us for our future.

Christians have been given power through the Holy Spirit who dwells in them to obey the Heavenly Father, giving no place to the plot of the devil. When we **submit ourselves to God, and resist the devil and he will flee from you. (James 4:7)**

Our enemy becomes powerless in our lives when we submit to our heavenly father.

(1 John 4:4) **. . . greater is He that is in you, than he that is in the world.**

You have help to guide you on this Christian journey, to keep you from slipping, falling, and deviating from the path of obedience.

(Isaiah 59:19) **. . . When the enemy shall come in like a flood, the Spirit of the LORD shall lift up a standard against him.** The Holy Spirit is always leading and guiding you into all truth, revealing the word of God if you do not grieve him. The Holy Spirit has a work to perform through you! He is always trying to get your attention! He is always near, guiding you back to the right path of the Father. Remember sin breeds more sin, so we must walk in the Spirit and obey Gods'

heavenly directives. This will activate the Holy Spirit in our lives and bring the results of holiness.

(Galatians 5:16-17) **This I say then, walk in the Spirit, and ye shall not fulfill the lust of the flesh.** (Self-examination: we must always put our flesh in check!)

(Galatians 5:19-21) **Now the works of the flesh are manifest, which are these; Adultery, fornication, uncleanness, lasciviousness, Idolatry, witchcraft, hatred, variance, emulations, wrath, strife, seditions, heresies, envyings, murders, drunkenness, reveling, and such like: of the which I tell you before, as I have also told you in time past, that they which do such things shall not inherit the kingdom of God.**

As a soldier, we must know what kind of enemy we are dealing with and figure out the devices, strategies, and different tactics that might come your way. The soldier must be in a state of readiness for sudden sneak attacks or unexpected rapid fire.

"To submit and resist is the power of submission unto God!"

(James 4:7) **Submit yourselves therefore to God. Resist the devil, and he will flee from you.**

This should be our reaction from an attack of the enemy: to meditate on the word of God and its application *("**Unto God, Submit and Resist**")*. This is what is needed to pull down strong holds. One who loves and trusts God completely will adhere to His holy directives and flawless instructions. True love dispels all doubts and fears, propelling one to push past all of life's concerns and circumstances that weigh a person down. True surrender is totally trusting God, submitting to His word and cast all your cares and everything that concerns you onto God.

(Psalm 55:22) Cast thy burden upon the Lord, and he shall sustain thee: he shall never suffer the righteous to be moved.

I realized that carrying heavy loads of pain and shame is futile; for only the burden bearer (Jesus) can lift this heavy task from us. Almighty God removes our burdens and hears our concerns when we release them to Him in prayer. When a believer in Christ submits to God, it is a surrender of their will to His will (authority), obeying His word. I once found it hard to deny myself. I always wanted to do my own thing. Now, as a child of God, I give up my own gratification and submit to the will of God. I resist the lies and temptation of the devil, and he flees. I take up my cross and follow Jesus.

(Matthew 16:24) Then Jesus said to his disciples, If any man will come after me, let him deny himself, and take up his cross, and follow me.

Our life is not our own, because we have been purchased and redeemed by Jesus! We have been adopted into His royal family. We must fortify ourselves daily by meditating on the word of God. We must be prepared and ready to withstand the attacks of our enemy by putting on the whole armor of God.

(Ephesians 6:10-11) Finally, my brethren, be strong in the Lord, and in the power of his might. Put on the whole armor of God that ye may be able to stand against the wiles of the devil. With God's armor, we are equipped for spiritual warfare, built up and ready for battle *(combat)*. Remember, evil is always present, trying to stop the traveler. He has unrestrained, diabolical, evil ambitions that constantly bombard our lives, never leaving us alone—no, not for a minute—for Satan is diligent, on his post 24 hours, 7 days a week, holding no punches, hurling fiery darts that aim to take us off the path of moral, godly standards. Once, I danced with the enemy and played Russian roulette with my life. I didn't consider the cost. I never realized that my decisions were leading me down the path of self-destruction.

The nightlife of sin seemed glamorous, enticing, and exciting. I hung out in clubs, especially on ladies' night. The intoxicating liquor was at my disposal. In those dark places, there was always a subtle, influential person who was willing and able to introduce me to the next level of sin. It was like opening Pandora's Box of seductive choices.

The "thou shalt not" of the "Ten Commandments" was taught in my home. My siblings and I were not strangers to the very profound words given by God to Moses in *Exodus 20:1-17* on Mount Sinai, written by God on two tablets.

The question is, "What makes a person choose to do the opposite of what they were taught?" As a youth in church, I learned the Ten Commandments. I can recall a time when my behavior was the opposite of what I was taught. One of the commandments of God states, "Thou shall not steal!" I knew it was wrong to take anything that I did not pay for, but on Sundays my mother would give us permission to attend church with our neighbor, who went to church every Sunday. Mom would give us change to put in the church offering, but when the offering tray came around, we did not put all the money into the tray, only a small amount of change. I kept most of the money, and after church we walked home without adult supervision and stopped at the local store to buy candy. Most of it ended up in my pockets. Oh my!

Sinful behaviors were displayed after attending Sunday services. Not obeying what I was taught, I did not have any remorse for my actions. Some of us local kids had the seeds of deception sown in an early part of our lives, and sin continued to grow. In my teens, I still misbehaved with "immoral action," doing things that others instructed me to do on a mission called "find and take".

I believe sinful conduct should be exposed and then eradicated from one's life. In order for change to come, one must have a genuine desire to repent of their sins. To continue on the same destructive path, doing the same thing and thinking that something good will be the outcome, is the definition of insanity (nothing good comes from wrongdoing).

When I think about the word "temptation," what comes to mind is a misleading plan of lustful desires. The world exposed me to many tempting things. I should have run for the hills and hid. However, on a serious note, the choices made were my own. I am reminded of this old adage: "If you play with fire, you will get burned." I am now aware of the dangers of playing with fire *(pyrophobia)* and the deceitful ploys of the tempter. The devil uses what God says you should not do, falsifying or justifying something wrong as being right. The devil is a liar! His scheme of deception is to poison you, so that you die and never become spiritually alive. He wants you to be toxic and infect others, using people who are living and obeying his sinful directives—who are nothing but recruiters, poisoning others who will also produce devilish, disobedient, and ungodly people. *(John 8:44)* **Ye are of your father the devil, and the lusts of your father ye will do. He was a murderer from the beginning, and abode not in the truth, because there is no truth in him. When he speaks a lie, he speaks of his own: for he is a liar, and the father of it.** Everyone has a free will to choose right from wrong. We have the power to say "no" and run from temptation.

"Ungodly Motives displayed"

I want to talk about a person who sells drugs for a moment. They are extortionists, influenced by greed and selfishness. They have chosen the path of deception. The seller of drugs buys into this game of quick or easy money. They sell drugs which will destroy and kill people, all for material gain and profit. I heard some even say this is what they had to do, in order to survive or to get out of the "hood." But when you sell drugs to people, you have participated in the plan of the enemy. Many people have died from indulging in illicit substances, and some have even taken a life. Anyone who does not have the love of God always will be driven by deception and defeated to degradation.

The Second Commandment of God is unto our fellow man: **(Matthew 22:39-40) And the second is like unto it, Thou shalt love thy neighbor as thyself. On these two commandments hang all the law and the prophets.** When a person hurts another human being, they are breakers of this great commandment of God!

People who sell drugs profit from the pain and misery of others. They feed off of their out-of-control lifestyles, cravings, and addictions, which consist of a daily consumption of drugs and the need to get more by any means necessary. The dealer does not care about the person or who else is affected by their sickness.

There are some people who are filled with hate and envy, which can lead them to dishonor others or cause harm. There are other ungodly behaviours, which include forsaking the poor and needy, and others have a prejudiced attitude, commit adultery, and even sexism.

The word of God states clearly how mankind ought to treat others.

{Luke 6:31} **And as ye would that men should do to you, do ye also to them likewise.**

The Apostle Paul's epistle to the Romans states: *(Romans 13:8-9)* **Owe no man anything, but to love one another: for he that loves another hath fulfilled the law. For this,**

Thou shalt not commit adultery, Thou shalt not kill, Thou shalt not steal, Thou shalt not bear false witness, Thou shalt not covet; and if there be any other commandment, it is briefly comprehended in this saying, namely, <u>Thou shalt love thy neighbor as thyself.</u>

To all the dysfunctional travelers, the Bible states in *Romans 13:10:* **Love works no ill to his neighbor: therefore love is the fulfilling of the law.**

Sin will keep you from God, for He is a Holy God and hates any sin that man indulges in. Thanks be to God that he loves the sinner but not the sin. His Holy Word clearly states the guidelines for mankind to live a successful life. Deep down inside of man, there is an inner awareness of right and wrong. God has placed inside of every person he created a moral conscience. Therefore, we are held accountable for our own actions.

WHOSE SIDE ARE YOU ON?

The bible clearly states, "You cannot serve two masters"! *(Matthew 6:24)* **No man can serve two masters: for either he will hate the one, and love the other; or else he will hold to the one, and despise the other: Ye cannot serve God and mammon.**

There isn't a neutral zone. You're on the Lord's side or the devil's! We cannot have our cake and eat it, too! In **Revelation 3:16**, it says, "**So then because thou art lukewarm, and neither cold nor hot, I will spew thee out of my mouth.**"

Mankind has two choices in this world: you can be a child of God or a follower of the fallen one, the devil. It's your decision.

And if it seem evil unto you to serve the LORD, choose you this day whom ye will serve; whether the gods which your fathers served that were on the other side of the flood, or the gods of the Amorites, in whose land ye dwell: but as for me and my house, we will serve the LORD. (Joshua 24:15)

I believe if I took a poll, asking the question, "Do you think you will go to heaven without being a disciple of Christ?" some would answer unequivocally "yes"! Well this concept is the wrong answer. For Satan brings a false religion, saying you can live an unholy life, as long as you attend church services and follow the traditions of the denomination. This is untrue, for I have heard people say these things to justify their moral goodness. I give alms and charity to the poor and needy, and not greedy, and I attend church regularly. I haven't killed anybody, and the list of excuses is endless. They provide an extensive résumé on why heaven should be theirs, based on their perspective. The indictment is self-righteousness, relying on their own ability, which will not cut it for you.

Evil works are exposed on the news every day before our eyes. Crime, murder, robbery, drugs, sex, poverty, greed, hunger, wars, sickness, prejudice, injustice, and the list goes on.

Fleshly behavior, ungodly desires and ambitions are in stark contrast with a Holy God who will judge the intentions of the mind and heart. God gives the enemy the authority when we play in the playground called "disobedience." It is our responsibility to change and to accept God's help through his son Jesus Christ to refuse sin and to obey Almighty God!

(Galatians 6:7-8) **Be not deceived; God is not mocked: for whatsoever a man sows, that shall he also reap. For he that sows to his flesh shall of the flesh reap corruption; but he that sows to the Spirit shall of the Spirit reap life everlasting.**

The word "Christian" means Christ-like, and Jesus is our example. He submitted himself to the will of his Father as his earthly demise was before him, bearing the sins of the world. It was a heavy burden placed upon him. We must learn from Jesus, who lived a life totally submitted unto the will of his Father. We must follow a life of obedience unto our heavenly father God, as well. When the going got tough for Jesus, he proceeded to pray to the Father, and we must have that same act of submission.

(Matthew 26:39) **And he went a little farther, and fell on his face, and prayed, saying, O my Father, if it be possible, let this cup pass from me: nevertheless not as I will, but as you will but as thou wilt.**

Poem:

True Love:

True love never comes and goes, true love stays and grows.

True love develops and increases in time.

Strong feelings of affection bring joyful tears from my eyes.

Like a mother's love, so caring and deserving.

My voice I raise! Praise!

True love always prevails and never fails.

It only goes God's way!

True love is heavenly, given to all who have repented of sin and received Jesus Christ as their Lord and Savior.

For ye have not received the spirit of bondage again to fear; but ye have received the Spirit of adoption, whereby we cry, Abba, Father. (Romans 8:15)

CHAPTER 3

God's love for all humanity!
(Agape Love)

**(John 3:16) For God so loved the world that he gave
his only begotten Son, that whosoever believeth in
him should not perish, but have everlasting life.**

The one and only true and living God has a love for all mankind,
a people that he created— an unconditional love which no one
deserves—for his love towards man is not that they loved God but
that he loved us and sent his Son as an atoning sacrifice for humanity's
sins.

God is love, and his love is unfailing, His decision to love a sinful
and unfaithful people is incomprehensible. *(Romans 5:8)* **But God
commends his love toward us, in that, while we were yet sinners,
Christ died for us.**

Who can perceive this eternal agape love? Only those reciprocal individuals of the Gospel of Jesus Christ, for without God being the head of their life, one will only see what love is through erroneous forms of human affections, such as being a good citizen, generosity in giving, marital things, or engaging in sexual relations. God's directives concerning marriage are crystal clear, which He has stated is only between men and women. Also, there are acts of abnormal behaviors, selfishness, controlling spirits, conditional love, insensitive abandonment, mental, physical, and verbal abuse, and spewing out of one's mouth "I love you."

(1 John 4:8-10) He that loves not knows not God; for God is love. In this was manifested the love of God towards us, because that God sent His only begotten Son into the world that we might live through him. Herein is love, not that we loved God, but that he loved us, and sent his Son to be the propitiation for our sins.

Those who have rejected the love of God, I say to all mankind this day, who have living breath pumping throughout their bodies: you are still afforded and given this great, divine, merciful opportunity to be reconciled unto Jesus Christ.

By accepting Jesus Christ as my Lord and Savior, I have experienced God's agape love. He has graciously provided this way of sin escape, spreading his love toward mankind through covenants, dispensations, and ultimately the propitiatory sacrifice of Jesus.

Only through His resurrection and ascension we become sons and daughters of God's unconditional love through faith. My encounter with God's love came to fruition. The very essence of this truth I ponder on, knowing that my unworthiness and undeserving life has been graciously forgiven, and I have received a second chance. All because of God's love for me, now my life has true meaning and divine purpose.

November 4, 1990 is my spiritual birthday *(born again)*. I can vividly remember on that day when the very presence of God expelled the darkness of sin from my life, removing the guilt and shame of sin, and replacing it with grace, love, and mercy. This great spiritual, divine encounter with God Almighty permeated my very being. I was in awe of God's forgiveness, knowing now that there is no greater love than the one who created me. No one can ever love me like my heavenly Father has. At the lowest level of my life, he was right there—not with an "I told you so" or condemning me, just true, abiding comfort and love, always making a way of escape, so I can make a conscious decision to accept his love.

God used my husband at a pivotal time in my life, when my life decisions had spiraled out of control. My husband's love for me was guided by almighty God, for he had just rededicated his life back to God. This was after the passing of his mother, which weighed heavily on his heart. God guided him back to his true love, God. He was determined to share the love of God is with me, so he proceeded to water the seeds that were already planted in my life.

This message of love was presented to me in such a plain but yet profound way *(my honey was preaching the Gospel to me)*. If I placed a title on this message, it would be "You're out of order with God", for he said, and I quote: "You are the devil's advocate, and you need to get right with God." Some would say that these words were very harsh, but those very words pierced into my heart, melting away some of the darkness that held me bound. Yes, I got upset and was deeply offended, saying to myself, "This man needs to leave my mother's house," but sometimes you have to take off the kid gloves and use bare knuckles to make an impact (keeping it 100% real talk). No shortcuts for truth, which is an agent for change. You have to tell it like it is! God showed His unconditional love and mercy, in spite of my folly, when I almost lost my life in a terrible car accident. Without God on my side, I was destined for ruin, on my way to a burning hell. I was very stubborn, hard headed, and totally worldly, bound up in a very explosive state of mind, and change was truly a needed thing for me. My husband was an agent of that change and a beacon of light through the aid of the Holy Spirit of God.

Hubby did not just leave me with those words, he also gave me the only answer that pricked at my heart. He told me his mother share with him how one could be born again, which was the prerequisite for receiving Christ as Lord and Savior [if you want to be saved, pray]: "Lord, please save me and come into my heart." I heard these words, and they truly stayed with me. After entering into my room, I turned on the television, and the show was on called *Highway to Heaven*, and I began to cry. I said to myself, "Lord, please save me. Come into my heart," for I truly knew I needed God, for he alone could help me. I proceeded to put legs to my faith, instead of coming home drunk and laying in bed with a hangover. While my family religiously went to church, a feeling of conviction to want change was tugging at my heart.

On November 4, 1990 this day will always be easily remembered, because it was also my husband's birthday. I went to church with my husband and daughter, and the sermon was about the people of Sodom and Gomorrah. In this message, I learned that they were polluted with sin and ungodly behaviors. This story was insightful to me, due to sin in my own life, for the people of Sodom and Gomorrah were judged by God. He heard the outcry against these people who rejected His love and who were living sinful and wicked lives. His response was to judge them according to righteousness, because of the sin and wickedness. God hates sin, but he loves the sinner and renders judgment unto them. A good example is a parent who is responsible for their offspring. When a child is disobedient, they must be punished, and this is tough love.

The message was very clear as I listened to the preached word of God brought forth by his minister on that particular Sunday: God's love for people who love him and obey him, as they would escape the fire of Sodom and Gomorrah. My heart was open to the truth of God's word; I felt this message was tailor made for me, because I wanted to escape from my own life that was filled with sin. I made up my mind and believed in my heart that I wouldn't turn back to the ruins of my life, for that was not an option.

After Sunday service, still pondering on the preached word of God, my husband and I were invited to our sister in-law's house to pray for my husband's brother. He was not feeling well. All who were gathered together formed a prayer circle. Someone started off praying for all the members of the family who were present in the circle. With my eyes closed and head down, I was holding my husband's hand and daughter's.

Please allow me the privilege to bring you into this great earth-shattering day that changed my life forever. I'll set the stage as a playwright. Scene—Act One: "Redemption on the Rise." As I began to pray within, "God, I know we came here to pray for my brother in-law, but will you please touch him, and please save me?" Suddenly, the presence of the Holy Spirit came upon me, feeling this enormous heat all over my body. I did not understand what was truly happening to me. All of a sudden, I wanted to let go of my husband's hand. I did not want to lose my composure or my coolness by not having it all together. I felt like I had to vomit. While all this was happening, a logical thought came across my mind. I believed that it was the food which we had eaten earlier: White Castle burgers with onion rings. I was trying to justify the reason why I was feeling the way I did during prayer. The White Castle burgers were not the case; the burger thought was just a lying distraction. The distraction did not work, for the power of God was undeniably all over me, deep down in the pit of my stomach. I felt a heavy dryness in my mouth, going through the motions like I was vomiting but nothing came out. Later, I understood that I was being purged by the power of almighty God!

In *The All Nations Complete Christian Dictionary*, the meaning for purge is "to clean or purify, from sin, guilt, or defilement." I [Ms. Cool!]—the power of the Holy Spirit had slayed me out on the living room floor, and my husband knew that Jesus had saved me and had come into my heart. He was saying "praise God!" Then I arose from the floor, born again as a new creature in Christ.

(2 Corinthians 5:17) Therefore if any man be in Christ, he is a new creature: old things are passed away; behold, all things are become new.

As we walked outside to go home, I looked up at the sky, and the clouds appeared as beautiful mountains; everything was lustrously bright. I am from Long Island, New York, and the fall seasons are breathtaking. I felt like a passenger staring out of the window, admiring the leaves on the trees and the leaves on the ground. I felt like a little kid "looking at the trees" with a new excitement. Everything looked so beautiful to me at 27 years old.

It was like being on earth for so many years and now seeing the world with a new perspective. The colors of the trees leaves, they were so amazing to me—like I had seen them for the first time. I had an awesome born again experience, for God's love is so real, and when you know him, you want to share it with everyone.

GOD'S LOVE MUST ALWAYS BE SHARED WITH OTHERS!

When we witness to others about God's love, we become a bridge with arms extended, truly caring for others. *(1 John 4:7)* **Beloved, let us love one another: for love is of God; and every one that loveth is born of God, and knoweth God.**

On my life's journey, I have encountered people who are desperately searching for a special ingredient called love that is missing in their lives. Many don't understand that love is an essential part of our entire DNA. We all are carriers of love. A newborn baby feels love at birth in the form of being cared for and nurtured, even in the mother's womb. Love is demonstrated in many forms of emotions, strong attractions, objects of affection, and desires.

When I think about what true love is, I think about God's love, which is never failing.

This word "love" has been mishandled in our society today, and many people have uttered these words "I Love You," yet they never meant a single word. They were only empty words.

Grievous and disappointing situations in one's life have polluted many people who were born to be a channel of God's love but were heartbroken individuals who have been used and abused and lied to, having low self-esteem, unsure of their potential in life. Confusion brings interference into this love factor—a dysfunctional family and an environment that's full of despair. Some have been harshly spoken to and ill treated by those who say they love them. It's a display of unfruitful substances that did not mirror true love. There is always a root cause and effect that takes place and forms into all kinds of problematic behavior.

It is critical to identify the source of such dysfunction planted earlier in a person's life that grows into a tree of discouragement by negative spoken words. There is an old saying I was accustomed to hearing growing up: *"Sticks and stones may break your bones, but words will never harm you."* Definitely, this saying is untrue. The words that come out of a person's mouth can be a tool for building or destroying the life of the hearer. *Biblical scripture States, (Ephesians 4:29)* **Let no corrupt communication proceed out of your mouth, but that which is good to the use of edifying, that it may minister grace unto the hearers.** This is a scripture that always stood out to me and brings an awareness of the importance of the power of words. There is a verse that speaks about the human body, the mouth, and the tongue: *(Proverbs 18: 21)* **Death and life are in the power of the tongue.**

People have succumbed to the negativity of inadequate dialogues which diminish the receiver's self-esteem. Many of the causes of inadequate self-esteem stem from a person's upbringing, and today some of these poisoning seed-planters wear the label "bully," which consists of taunting and spewing words that destroys a person's character.

And if that person is not strong enough to understand their own self-worth, this will cause collateral damages that can be explosive for the individual who is seeking social acceptance from their peers or colleagues. These hurtful experiences can be detrimentally painful in one's life when trying to please others.

"Looking for love in all the wrong places"

There are many who have the opportunity to sow good and meaningful love seeds toward others. Forming friendship or mutual acquaintances, associates, colleagues, and neighbors—we must not take relationships lightly, because we need each other. No one lives on an island alone.

"Twisted love portrayed by evil intent"

Anyone who verbally, physically, or mentally torments a person and then claims they love them is a sadist. Those who love wrongly have been wrongfully loved themselves. Just check out the root that it came from: spawning unproductive abuse and breeding contamination that is rotten to the core. These kinds of fruits are in need of God's love in their lives. If anyone chooses to stay in this state, they will totally miss out on what love is really all about.

"Fruit Bearing"

God is the giver of all true love that's pure and holy, without any blemishes. The Children of God will always display these characteristic traits, "and these characteristics are called the fruit of the spirit." *(Galatians 5:22-23)* **But the fruit of the Spirit is love, joy, peace, longsuffering, gentleness, goodness, faith, meekness, temperance: against such there is no law.** We are to love **God** and obey him, exemplifying his characteristics each and every day of our lives. *(Galatians 5:24-26)* **And they that are Christ's have crucified the flesh with the affections and lusts. If we live in the Spirit, let us also walk in the Spirit. Let us not be desirous of vain glory, provoking one another, envying one another.**

Showing brotherly love to our neighbor is of the utmost importance, and it is morally right to exhibit kindness, lending a helping hand when needed. These are the attributes of the Spirit, and they represent Christ's divine nature.

(1 John 3:17-18) **But whoso hath this world's good, and seeth his brother have need, and shutteth up his bowels of compassion from him, *how dwelleth the love of God in him*? My little children, let us not love in word, neither in tongue; but indeed and in truth.**

CHAPTER 4

"Man's Time on earth"—Tick Tock!

W hen a person is born into this world, it is the beginning of a new life, and then the clock begins to tick. Tick tock—every second, minute, and hour of the day! The very essence of man's time on earth has been divinely arranged—all having purpose and destiny with promise.

(Ecclesiastical 3:1-2) **To everything there is a season, and a time to every purpose under the heaven: A time to be born, and a time to die; a time to plant, and a time to pluck up that which is planted.**

God created time *(Genesis 1:14)*. On earth, he divided AM and PM for signs and seasons, yet he is a timeless God from everlasting to everlasting. God placed man in space and time, which was limitless without boundaries. Man's transgression altered time, placing him on a chronological clock. Now, we are responsible to maintain our time more efficiently, because our life here on earth depends on our use of it. We all are given an expiration date, and sin will ultimately stop your time clock from ticking.

I speak from experience and truly understand this, for one night I almost went from the cradle to the grave (figuratively speaking). Upon visiting a graveyard, one encounters the head stone, which has a person's name, **D.O.B (Date of Birth) and D.O.D (Date of Death).** The hyphen separates the two, which is your legacy, your contribution to society, contribution to humanity, your Christian ethics, your church family, and inheritance. As long as you're breathing and above ground, you are marking time. Each of us has 24 hours a day, and the question is how wisely do you spend your time? If you abuse it, time will surely tell on you.

In the late 80s, playing Russian roulette with my time, burning the candle at both ends, livin *la vida loca (crazy).* My time in this world was almost snuffed out. One night I recall in particular: I was going to work. In my youthful years, I enjoyed drinking and getting high—bad-habited, I truly needed to be free from such ungodly substance. I told my husband that I was going to stop drinking and was giving it up.

But on that peculiar night of temptation, none of my co-workers or I could imagine what would take place on that night. As I arrived at my place of employment, the supervisor said that there is beer and food in the back. It was party time at the job! I indulged in habitual drinking with some of the employees *(if drugs and alcohol didn't take me out, the car accident I was in would have).* Leaving the job during lunch time, still on the clock, I wound up in the hospital, sustaining injuries consisting of broken neck, hip, right arm, right leg in four places, a fractured pelvis, and two front teeth that were cracked. To add insult to injuries, I was placed in a halo for support of my neck for three months. I could have been paralyzed—or worse, dead—but God extended my time, giving me an opportunity to repent from my sins. By divine intervention, reconciliation would be at the door of my heart.

(Tick-Tock).

Satan still was beating my time. In other words, he had a stronghold on me. I wasn't ready to become a Christian. I was hospitalized for two and a half months. I woke up in the hospital to see my mother's pastor, Pastor Hazards *(ironic to say the least)* with his head down, praying.

He never really said anything to me but smiled and prayed. Also, several other Christians would visit me and kept me in prayer, yet my focus was on returning to the club scene and dying my hair blonde. Wow! Just the thought of my mindset at that time makes me say, "Oh my." Time was winding up, and look at what I was focusing on. Released from the hospital, wearing a halo to support my neck and spine and a full leg brace, I was in need of Godly assistance, I was unaware of this key component which would heal my broken life. At this devastating time in my life, I went from being in a wheelchair then to a walker. For a period of time, my daily schedule of events consisted of physical therapy. I needed to learn how to walk anew. The clock was still moving [tick tock], but it was not over. The opportunity for eternal life was still present in time for me.

"Christians are under construction"

The important reminder for all believers is to understand is that Christians are "**still under construction**". *(Philippians 1:6)* **Being confident of this very thing, that he which hath begun a good work in you will perform it until the day of Jesus Christ:**

Construction is the very process of building something, and time is a factor allocated for completion. When anything is being built, blueprints are required, and an idea is formulated. A vision is then put into action, and all of the planning, preparation, and building materials make a **solid foundation**. Knowing all the intricacies involved in completing a building, a builder can testify and explain about the structures, the roof, and the walls—how everything is joined together by design.

Consequently, my daughter is buying her first home. In the process of being built, we went to look at a model home, in order to choose the one that's ideal for her family. To see all the work being done on the homes and the mental gymnastics that it takes to choose the color, stairs, wooden floors or title, and all of the extra amenities, I came to the realization that the children of God are similar. Father God has designed, refined, and formulated our very existence as the church—presently unfinished but still under construction.

The Apostle Paul tells the church at Philippi that he *(God)*, who has begun a good work in them, shall get the job done. *(Philippians 1:6) Being confident of this very thing, that he which hath begun a good work in you will perform it until the day of Jesus Christ.*

He wrote to these church members while he was incarcerated, enduring suffering for the cause of Christ. Paul encouraged this body of believers that they were partners in the gospel with him. He wrote a thank you letter expressing his joy in what God was accomplishing through them. The church *("The Temple of the Holy Spirit")* is still under construction *("We are a work in progress").* The Apostle made the church aware that God doesn't only start a good work in us, but He will finish what he started. Guiding our very steps each and every day, tick tock the clock is still moving.

"Death Trap"

CHAPTER 5

Unprepared – And
Prepared Traveler!

A dventures are experiences that one has as they make their
pilgrimage through life on earth, which can sometimes be very
exciting, risky, unusual, and even dangerous. Have you ever
taken a risk, doing whatever you want to do, having no boundaries or
limitations? Many people are in this very state of mind today. I can
testify to taking risks, making knee-jerk decisions without concrete
directions, living day by day. I was unaware of my purposes in this
world, being an *"unprepared traveler"* —a carrier of many ungodly
worries and carrying baggage with an overweight stamp, paying a hefty
price.

The manufacturer, God has given me this great, awesome task to write
this book. This is a great opportunity to reach someone who is willing to

see vicariously the life of a traveler who is heaven bound share personal testimonies as a traveler who once was adventurous, heading in the wrong direction as a sinner, misguided, driven by worldly desires, being spiritually dead, without God's abundant love in my life! I was living an unprepared, unrelenting life at that time. I was not a receiver of the truth of God's word. Sin in my life was truly manifested and seen as behavioral choice consisting of me, myself and I. Heaven's destination was not an important factor for me. Being young and immature, the only thing that truly mattered was partying all the time!

People who say that they want to go to heaven but are not willing to investigate the infallible word of God are considered unprepared travelers for the journey. In order for one to get prepared, one must get rid of all the junk in their trunk and re-pack to unclutter your life. The greatest sin imaginable is denying the only way to God (blasphemy). A person who is an unprepared traveler looks at this from a non-spiritual perspective. Unprepared travelers have titles such as ***unnecessary, unsecured, unsuccessful, unhealthy, unsure, unfaithful, unhappy, unclean, unfruitful, and not positive***. These attributes are poisonous baggage.

I thank God that I am no longer a carrier of such patterns of destruction. I was on a quest with dreams and aspirations, which were momentarily put on hold because of my poor choices that crippled my potential. Now, my life has been changed, and I am heaven bound, a carrier of a born again life which reveals a new creature in Christ. *(2 Corinthians 5:17-18)* **Therefore if any man be in Christ, he is a new creature: old things are passed away; behold, all things are become new.**

As you can see in my testimony, I had to check myself before I wrecked myself totally. I was like a car wreck, busted, broken up, and twisted, in need of total repair and maintenance.

Ask yourself a question about your life journey: what have you received or retained if you spend your whole life preparing for the things of this world, be it jobs, money, school, homes, family, cars, and many other things which are needed in this earth, but when you depart from this world you take nothing with you? What good is all of this material wealth or inheritance to leave for loved ones and gain the whole world but lose out on opportunities that God graciously afforded to you through Jesus to receive eternal inheritance (life)?

In the Bible, there is a scripture that speaks to us about the love of money being the root of all evil. This is when man puts financial gain before God, excluding Him from their life, loving material things more than God! *(1 Timothy 6:10)* **For the love of money is the root of all evil: which while some coveted after, they have erred from the faith, and pierced themselves through with many sorrows.**

These perishable things will fade away, because they are temporary. This should really make one contemplate strongly about what or who they are trusting in. What are you really storing up for here on earth? One would purchase a burial plot, coffin, or headstone, and you might have thoughts of what church you want your service to be at, plus who will preside over your funeral.

We set up insurance policies, a will, and an inheritance delegated for our loved ones in the event of our demise, yet you never made provisions for the journey to heaven. Everything else took precedence while you had breath in your body. News flash! A person who has not accepted Jesus

Christ as their Lord and Savior is an ***Un-prepared Traveler***, dying outside of Christ. Their service is called a funeral for the dead without any future hope, but the ***Prepared traveler***, who received Jesus Christ, their service is called going home, an event of joyful bliss *(eternal life)*. *(2 Corinthians 5:8)* **We are confident, I say, and willing rather to be absent from the body, and to be present with the Lord.**

"The Dead in Christ Shall Rise!

(1 Thessalonians 4:13-16) **But I would not have you to be ignorant, brethren, concerning them which are asleep, that ye sorrow not, even as others which have no hope. For if we believe that Jesus died and rose again, even so them also which sleep in Jesus will God bring with him. For this we say unto you by the word of the Lord, that we which are alive and remain unto the coming of the Lord shall not prevent them which are asleep. For the Lord himself shall descend from heaven with a shout, with the voice of the archangel, and with the trump of God: and the dead in Christ shall rise first:**

Now I want to talk to you a little bit about ***A Prepared Traveler***, who is fully equipped and ready at all times for their expected trip, in which they have gathered together all the necessary things to have a successful trip. When one is taking a trip by vehicle, they need to make all the necessary preparations, such as money, maps, GPS, hotel reservation, a full tank of gas, spare tire, car maintenance, cell phone, snack box, luggage, and a first aid kit, equipping them for a successful trip.

In the Old Testament book of Joshua, this man of God was Moses' assistant minister and eventually became his successor. He was given assurance by God after the death of Moses. The LORD spoke to Joshua, and here is how I interpret it, "Get yourself up and put aside your sad state of mind, for you have places to go, people to lead, and there is much work to be done! For surety, you will achieve all you are to do, and everywhere you go, *I got you*, Joshua. Even as I was with Moses I will be with you." *(Joshua 1: 1-2)*

(Joshua 1:5) **There shall not any man be able to stand before thee all the days of thy life: as I was with Moses, so I will be with thee: I will not fail thee, nor forsake thee.**

"Meditate on God and stay focused"

When a child of God is obedient and has a daily meditation posture, studying the word of God, this is a portal for the believer to obtain spiritual growth and good success.

(Psalm 119:15) **I will meditate in thy precepts, and have respect unto thy ways.**

(Joshua 1:8) **This book of the law shall not depart out of thy mouth; but thou shalt meditate therein day and night, that thou mayest observe to do according to all that is written therein: for then thou shalt make thy way prosperous, and then thou shalt have good success.**

A prepared traveler is one who is totally successful because of the ability of their God, and they are prepared and equipped for the journey. One is never alone, being guided by the Holy Spirit [comforter], the promise of the Father *(God)*.

(Acts 1:8) **But ye shall receive power, after that the Holy Ghost is come upon you: and ye shall be witnesses unto me both in Jerusalem,**

and in all Judaea, and in Samaria, and unto the uttermost part of the earth.

The traveler has been given help for the journey, for he will abide with the born again traveler forever. Note: don't grieve him. He is the Spirit of truth, the comforter, who leads and guides them into all truth to a prepared place for a prepared people! *(John 14:1)* **Let not your heart be troubled: ye believe in God, believe also in me. In my Father's house are many mansions: If it were not so, I would have told you. I go to prepare a place for you.**

CHAPTER 6

Lost and Wandering Traveler!

(Luke 19: 10) **For the Son of man is come to seek and to save that which was lost.**

When I ponder on this word "lost," the ramifications of it is clear to me. Someone who is in this state is unable to find their own way out. KJV Dictionary Definition: to wander is to rove; to ramble here and there without any certain course or object in view.

"Three states of being lost"

(1). Physically – nowhere to be found, missing

(2). Mentally – disorders of the mind.

(3). Spiritually – separation from God because of sin

The validation of this statement in *Luke 19:10* is solidified in the fact that the *"Son of man is come to seek and save the lost"*. The purpose of Jesus' coming was to seek and to save that which is lost in the sense of direction and condition. The course of one's life consumed by the sin dilemma would render them lost.

One who is spiritually lost is considered disconnected from God.

(1 Corinthians 2:14) But the natural man receives not the things of the Spirit of God: for they are foolishness unto him: nether can he know them, because they are spiritually discerned.

Someone who is wandering is roaming around bewildered, looking at life with an "I don't care anymore" attitude *(pessimistic)*, having no true purpose or plan, just existing. All mankind was born in sin and shaped in iniquity; they are spiritually dead and unable to hear or understand, for God's word which is spirit and truth. The acronym for *Bible is: B-basic I-instruction B-before L-leaving E-earth"* to guide and deliver them from their sinful state of mind.

Spiritually, mankind was lost, in need of an escape path, which is only available through a repented life, accepting of Jesus Christ as their Lord and Savior. He is the only one who came to help those who are lost.

(Matthew 18: 11) For the Son of man is come to save that which was lost.

(John 3:3) Jesus answered and said unto him, Verily, verily, I say unto thee, Except a man be born again, he cannot see the kingdom of God.

(John 6:40) And this is the will of him that sent me, that everyone which seeth the Son, and believeth on him, may have everlasting life: and I will raise him up at the last day.

The Gospel of Luke gives us one of the parables of Jesus of the prodigal (Lost son). *(Luke 15:11-22)* **And he said, A certain man had two sons: And the younger of them said to his father, Father, give me the portion of goods that falleth to me. And he divided unto them his living. And not many days after the younger son gathered all together, and took his journey into a far country, and there wasted his substance with riotous living. And when he had spent all there arose a mighty famine in that land; and he began to be in want.**

In this story, a father's younger son wanted his inheritance before his time. He had the "I want it now" syndrome. His father knew that his son must learn on his own *("life experiences")*, and yes he did receive his inheritance. This younger son chose to do his own thing, which would lead him on a path of wasting his wealth in riotous living. Some would say he was living large *(big baller)*, but his poor decisions had no limits or boundaries. He had much and spent it until it was all gone. I can just imagine how he must have felt. I can relate because of once having this state of mind, unsure of what I was going to do when facing hard times. When you don't have a clue how to deal with tough circumstances, challenges, and failing, disappointment sets in. Depression and fear—all kinds of escalating emotions come crashing in. I just believe depression caused him for a period of time to stay away from those who loved and could help him. He ended up doing menial jobs, feeding swine, and he also desired to eat what the pigs received for food (slop), for no one cared enough to give him anything to eat. I believe that he had a failed perspective, being at the bottom of the bottom, but glory to our God he came to his senses, and the realization of his living conditions gave him a wakeup call. He came to himself. When your life spins out of order, and you have no control, you must come to the realization that you are in dire need of help and should never isolate yourself, for things will only get worse—not better.

(Luke 15:17-19) **And he came to himself, he said, How many hired servants of my fathers have bread enough and to spare, and I perish with hunger! I will arise and go to my, father, and say unto him, Father, I have sinned against heaven, and before thee. And am no more worthy to be called thy, son: make me as one of thy hired servants.**

In order for anyone to come to the realization of their dilemma, one must critically acknowledge their state of being, which causes one to observe objectively and subjectively. You must have a purpose and a plan for changing your circumstances and proceed in accomplishing this resolution. You must fortify and reassure yourself that you are under construction and that the foundation you are building upon is a sure one. *(1 Corinthians 3:11)* **For other foundation can no man lay than that is laid, which is Jesus Christ.**

(2 Timothy 2:19) **Nevertheless the foundation of God stands sure, having this seal, The Lord knows them that are his. And, Let everyone that names the name of Christ depart from iniquity.**

"Recovery steps for the lost and wandering person"

1. Forgive yourself and others: Lack of forgiveness can filter like poison traveling through your veins, body, mind, and soul, causing a state of bitterness.

(Matthew 6:14-15) **For if ye forgive men their trespasses, your heavenly Father will also forgive you: But if ye forgive not men their trespasses, neither will your Father forgive your trespasses.**

(Colossians 3:13) **Forbearing one another, and forgiving one another, if any man have a quarrel against any: even as Christ forgave you, so also do ye.**

2. Acknowledgment of sins: King David, in the Book of Psalms, admits the truth of his breaking of God's law, sinning against Him. *(Psalm 51:3)* **For I acknowledge my transgressions: and my sin is ever before me.**
3. Repent: turn around and let change over take you. *(Acts 3:19)* **Repent you therefore, and be converted, that your sins may be blotted out, when the times of refreshing shall come from the presence of the Lord.**
4. Faith must be in the very DNA of a person who is willing to believe what they cannot see with their eyes. Not knowing how things are going to work out in your life, we must have faith in God! He alone will work it all out. For faith, works is a necessary ingredient that will propel you out of your distresses.

(Hebrews 11:1) **Now faith is the substance of things hope for, the evidence of things not seen.** God is pleased when we activate our faith in Him!

(Hebrews 11:6) **But without faith it is impossible to please him: for he that cometh to God must believe that he is, and that he is a rewarder of them that diligently seek him.**

5. Forget those things that are behind you! Not letting your past control your today, get over it. If one does not put things in their proper place, there will be a catastrophic ripple effect called distractions, holding up God's plans for your life.

(Philippians 3:13) **Brethren, I count not myself to have apprehended: but this one thing I do, forgetting those things which are behind, and reaching forth unto those things which are before.**

None of us have it all together, no not one, for we all fall short—no such thing as a perfect person. *(Romans 3:10)* **As it is written, there is none righteous, no, not one.** We are truly determined to reach our goals, for our past is behind us, and our prize is ever before us.

6. Proceeding forward: Sometimes, when one is proceeding forward, this very movement can also consist of a push *(**P**ush, **U**ntil, **S**omething, **H**appens)* or press forward past the pressure of life's circumstances. Hard times should iron out the wrinkles in life. In the natural, when ironing a garment full of wrinkles, you use a little starch and press the steam button for help, but, having a mind made up to wear this outfit, no other one will do!

(Galatians 3:27) **For as many of you as have been baptized into Christ have put on Christ.**

(Ephesians 4:24) **And that ye put on the new man, which after God is created in righteousness and true holiness.**

"Don't forget to put your war clothes on"! (Ephesians 6:11) **Put on the whole armor of God, that ye may be able to stand against the wiles of the devil.**

(Philippians 3:14) **I press toward the mark for the prize of the high calling of God in Christ Jesus.** Heaven bound and rejoicing, awaiting the day to answer the call of God.

The Parable of the Lost Son is a vivid picture of a recovery story, in which the son returns to his father's house and was greeted by a loving parent with expressions of happiness, rejoicing, and a grateful celebration with gifts presented unto him. *(Luke 15:22–24)* **But the father said to his servants, Bring forth the best robe, and put it on him: and put a ring on his hand, and shoes on his feet: And bring hither the fatted calf, and kill it; and let us eat, and be merry. For this my son was dead, and is alive again; he was lost, and is found. And they began to merry.**

When I was living a life of sin, I was out of order, with no limits nor boundaries, and lost, not knowing that I needed to be found—unaware of the path of eternal destruction. The truth of needing help was ever knocking at my heart, and I could not even comprehend it. If I was to paint a picture using everyday objects to explain the hindrances of sinful pleasure,

"Sin blockers" are blinders on one's eyes, so the perception is wrong. *"Spiritual death"* ear wax clogged the ear gate, such as ungodly music and dancing with sin in the enemy's camp.

The things I indulged in did not bring me any true happiness, rather a broken life, which was in need of total repair. For a sinful life will always keep one lost and wandering—always in need, searching for something or someone to heal the pain and heartaches. I was trying to fulfill the empty void in my life. The realization of what was missing was a true love connection,

(worship), which was lost from the beginning, due to man's disobedience in the garden, separating us from God.

A redirected life of despair is one who has truly repented, having godly sorrow for their wrongdoings via **Conversion**, for everyone who has not accepted the only way to God is lost in their sin nature! However, they can be found and delivered from such destitute atrocities which impacted me with great desire to see others that are separated from God be set free, as well. No more chains holding me, for those the Son set free are free indeed.

(John 8:36) **If the Son therefore shall make you free, ye shall be free in deed.**

The *All Nations the Complete Christian Dictionary for Home and School* gives this meaning for the word lost: that which cannot be found, unable to find one's way. I was spiritually lost, not able to find my way to God, but I was in his plan of recovery!

(Luke 19:10) **For the Son of man is come to seek and save that which was lost.**

CHAPTER 7

Roadside Assistance—Witnesses!

I t is a fact that automobile accidents occur every day. Some are broadcasted on the news, and the results of some of them are devastating: casualties or permanent injuries sustained with which become life-altering injuries.

When a collision occurs while one is driving, help is definitely needed. One must dial 911 and a police officer on duty will respond, ready to assist when called. They are here to protect and serve people and property by enforcing the laws *(order keepers)*. In an accident, one must remain at the scene of the accident, because many things take place in which medical emergency assistance *(Ambulance)* is required.

You must contact your insurance company to inform them of your involvement in an accident for insurance purposes. Take photos of the damage and all vehicles and property at the accident scene. If you can, obtain all identification. *(including insurance cards and license plate numbers)*. Gathering witnesses at the scene of the accident can be a plus if court litigation is needed.

After all of this, the assistance of a lawyer is needed. In 1988, I was in a serious car accident. My brother's ex-girlfriend at that time assisted me in obtaining legal representation. She made a phone call to a reputable law firm called *Daniel P. Buttafuoco & Associates*. She heard about his firm on a Christian radio station in Long Island, New York. I was not a Christian at the time, but I was very grateful for assistance, unaware that this time was all in the plan of Almighty God.

He sent unto me true witnesses to spiritually guide me *(carriers of the gospel of Jesus Christ)*. They planted seeds by deeds and words, exemplifying God's love, and others came and watered, who were laborers of the gospel of Jesus Christ. I sustained many physical injuries, including a broken neck, hip, and my right leg was broken in four places. I also had a fractured pelvis and broken left arm.

From looking at the photos, the vehicle I was in was split in half. It looked like two cars, instead of one. The lawyer informed me that I had a legitimate case, and he would represent me. I was in the hospital for two and a half months while healing physically.

Daniel P. Buttafuoco was also a believer of the gospel of Jesus Christ *(a man of God)* who was concerned about my spiritual needs. He knew that I needed Jesus as my Savior. Being at death's door without hope, intercessions were made continuously by the saints. Several ministers came to visit me, including a missionary from my mother's church. I will never forget her; she brought grapes and several other items. My mother's pastor made several visits to the hospital, as well. Being on sedative medication and going in and out of sleep, I would wake up several times and see Pastor Hazard sitting and praying at my bedside. He was a man of few words, very kind, quiet, and peaceful.

Witnessing

In the summer of 1992, my cousin Bucky took me to obtain my learner's permit. I was 29 years old. It was a long-overdue appointment. I was a late bloomer who was overcoming some fears that I had, due to a devastating car accident that I had been in. *(pulling down strongholds)* I was determined to achieve this permit and then eventually obtain my driver's license. My cousin was determined also to assist me in obtaining my permit. He knew that this was an enormous step. He understood what I had been through, sustaining a broken neck (which had to be fused together). It was so hard for me to turn my neck, but, with God, I achieved my goal of getting my permit. I eventually received my driver's license (thank God!). I had no idea that my cousin's journey on this earth was coming to an end. He was a young man and very dear to my heart. We were very close. Before he left this earth, he never mentioned anything about his ailment or what he was going through—that he was terminally ill. I sensed that something was going on with him, and he was deteriorating right before my eyes. My spiritual pilgrimage of a changed life was very evident to him. In the past, we would hang out and get high on illicit drugs, drink alcohol, and party in clubs. Our lives were headed in the wrong direction. At this time, however, my life had been turned around, and I was equipped to share the gospel of Jesus Christ to my cousin. I told him that he needed Jesus in his life and to look at how Jesus had turned my life around.

I told him how I almost died in a car accident, which was a devastating experience for me and my family. I told him that I was now a living testimony of the grace and mercy of God.

He was looking at a miracle right before his eyes. My cousin had informed me he was seeking God himself and attending church. He said he confessed with his mouth and believed that Jesus died and rose from the dead.

On another occasion we took a flight to California to visit one other relative, a close cousin who also was terminally ill. That was a hard time for both of us, as we were all so very close. For I knew this was a difficult visit for my cousin who traveled with me. We arrived at our family's house in California, this experience was so painful and heart-breaking. Seeing my younger cousin who I grew up with on his bed of affliction in so much pain. I didn't know what to say to him at the time. As I held back my tears, his sister told me to read the bible to him. I was surprisingly shocked at her request because she was of a different religious belief. My cousin was lying on his bed, unable to talk, he mumbled to me "Bible." Without any hesitation, I opened the bible and began to read scripture to him. Then I asked him, do you believe that Jesus died and rose from the grave for you? Barely able to speak, he mumbled yes and nodded his head. Both of my cousins passed away, and I believe they accepted Jesus as their Lord and Savior.

"A Christian testimony" is a powerful tool, a way to share the gospel of Jesus Christ. Redemption from death and recipient of a born again life.

(1 Timothy 2:6) "Who gave himself a ransom for all, to be testified in due time."

Enlightening the listener about their spiritual transformation, believers are the only reflection of Christ that people can tangibly see.

An effective witness is like a gardener who plants seeds in the ground and waters them, so the growth process begins. Seeds become filled with water and grow a root underground, and then it shoots upwards towards the sun.

I am reminded of my personal experience of hearing about God's love for me. At different times, people have sowed seeds (the word of God), giving me a spiritual road map that uprooted the wrong seeds and weeds that were choking the life out of me.

(1 Corinthians 3:6) **I have planted, Apollos watered; but God gave the increase.** As long as you have breath in your body, you have an opportunity to turn your life to God.

JESUS: ROADSIDE ASSISTANCE TO A MAN NAMED SAUL!

In the New Testament book of Acts, there was a man known by his Jewish name Saul. He was well trained in the Jewish Scriptures and tradition, studying under his teacher Gamaliel, a Pharisee doctor of Jewish Law – one who was held in great esteem by all Jews.

(Acts 22:3) **I am verily a man which am a Jew, born in Tarsus, *a city* in Cilicia, yet brought up in this city at the feet of Gamaliel, and taught according to the perfect manner of the law of the fathers, and was zealous toward God, as ye all are this day.**

Book knowledge without revelation from God is dead. The Scribes and Pharisees made themselves knowledgeable of the sacred writings of that time, but they had no true spiritual relationship with Almighty God, their creator. Saul of Tarsus' religion was Judaism; he accepted what he learned wholeheartedly, yet he was taught only having book knowledge – spiritually unequipped (without truth).

(1Corinthians 2:14) **But the natural man receiveth not the things of the Spirit of God: for they are foolishness unto him: neither can he know them, because they are spiritually discerned.**

(Romans 7:6) **But now we are delivered from the law, that being dead wherein we were held; that we should serve in newness of spirit, and not in the oldness of the letter.**

(2 Corinthians 3:6) **Who also hath made us able ministers of the New Testament; not of the letter, but of the spirit: for the letter kills, but the spirit giveth life.**

Saul was traveling to Damascus, the Capital of Syria *(Isaiah 7:8).* His purpose and assignment was to find Christians and persecute them with a religious zeal. He truly believed that he was doing the right thing for God, and no man could stop his pursuit of punishment. The people he would find would have been arrested, imprisoned, beaten, tortured – be they male or female, even children would be slaughtered (murder).

(Acts 9: 1-2) **And Saul, yet breathing out threatening and slaughter against the disciples of the Lord, went unto the high priest, And desired of him letters to Damascus to the synagogues, that if he found any of this way, whether they were men or women, he might bring them bound unto Jerusalem.**

Saul made a statement, **And I persecuted this way unto death, binding and delivering into prisons both men and women** *(Acts 22:4).* Which speak of the Christian religion (Christianity), and those who proclaim it. It is very important for us to see that Saul, an educated man of the Mosaic Law, thought he was operating in the will of God.

His misunderstanding of what he perceived to be truth caused him to persecute believers and take their innocent lives.

One day, Saul had an experience with Jesus which revealed the truth of his wrong interpretation of the scriptures. He found out he was absolutely in error – like many of us today who have erroneous doctrines and preconceived notions of theology!

They are in need of roadside assistance to redirect them on the road of the gospel of truth in Jesus Christ that leads to the pathway of eternal life.

(Acts 9:3-5) And as he journeyed, he came near Damascus: and suddenly there shined round about him a light from heaven: And he fell to the earth, and heard a voice saying unto him, Saul, Saul, why persecutest thou me? And he said, who art thou, Lord? And the Lord said, I am Jesus whom thou persecutest: it is hard for thee to kick against the pricks.

When Jesus shows up in someone's life, He makes a difference – an unforgettable, life-changing encounter that brings divine deliverance from death (sin), which separates one from God. Through faith in Jesus Christ, by the preached word of God, one embraces His unconditional love that He displayed on the cross. The power of His resurrection provided a way of escape from death; he arose, and now the one who receives him has risen, also. There are those who respond to the truth of the gospel. God's mercy and grace give hope for humanity— a bridge of hope that reaches far past prejudice, injustice, poverty, or sickness.

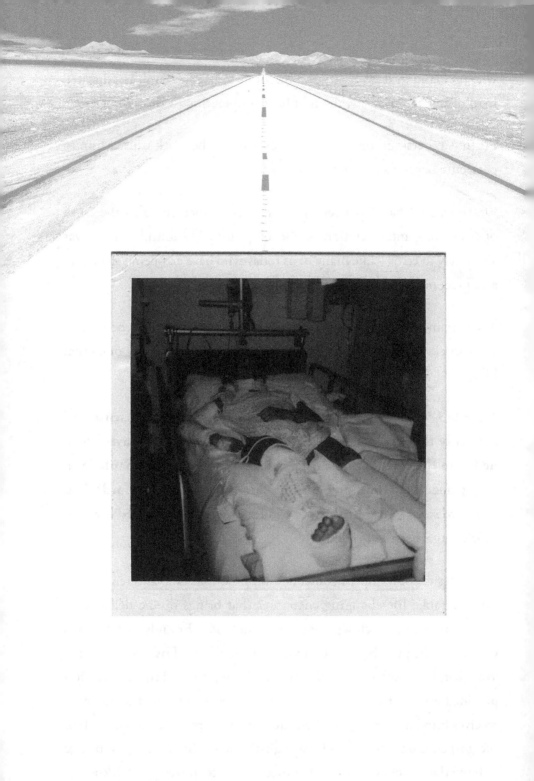

CHAPTER 8

U – Turns! Are Permitted!

One day, I and a friend went out of our town to attend a religious engagement. My friend drove; we were excited to fellowship with other Christians who would be at this function, and we wanted to arrive there on time. We were almost there it; was at night, and it started to rain. This was unfamiliar territory – nice neighborhood, but the rain was coming down harder. Without a clear focus, she ended up heading in the wrong direction. Thank God, we were able to make a U-turn before other cars came down the road. This was a scary situation, but we were safe. I believe that some of you who drive can relate to this (or maybe not). I did not anticipate this happening, but it was definitely something one must handle quickly, or there could have been a head-on collision.

Drivers, how do you feel about a no U-turn sign when you need to turn around and you can't? You must obey the traffic sign, following the rules and regulations of the road. You have to go out of the way to make the U-turn to head you back in the right direction. You must position the vehicle by signaling, then turning the steering wheel to make a complete U-turn. When a Christian has sin and turns away from Almighty God, just go ahead. U-turns are allowed, praise God. The Bible defines a person or a nation that falls back as backsliding. This was the term the prophets used to describe Israel's unfaithfulness to God. *(Isaiah 57:17)*

(Jeremiah 3:14) **Turn, O backsliding children, saith the LORD; for I am married unto you...** Israel truly had a broken relationship (fellowship) with the LORD by adhering to fleshly desires and immoral behavior. Some were even worshipping idols. They had forsaken and abandoned the truth they once believed. Religious abandonment is one who backslides and has deliberately chosen to turn backward spiritually, morally, and in religious practice.

The prophet Jeremiah spoke about hope for Israel, for they had turned away from the very precepts of God. *(Jeremiah 14:7)* **O LORD, though our iniquities testify against us, do thou it for thy name's sake: for our backslidings are many; we have sinned against thee.**

(Proverbs 14:14) The backslider in heart shall be filled with his own ways: and a good man shall be satisfied from himself.

Being a child of God is a great blessing that should not be taken lightly! It is a sad state of affairs when one of God's children gets disconnected from Him. Backslider, you are in need of a turnaround! Reconnect to your heavenly father! He is waiting with His arms open wide for you to return. *(Jeremiah 3:22)* **Return, ye backsliding children, and I will heal your backslidings. Behold, we come unto thee; for thou art the LORD our God.**

Israel refused to repent and return to their first love; they held onto their ungodly lifestyles. They were a people who were bent on backsliding, wow! Even today, many are determined to stay in a sinful position; they are bent on self-destruction.

(Jeremiah 8:4-7) Moreover thou shalt say unto them, Thus saith the LORD; Shall they fall, and not arise? shall he turn away, and not return? Why then is this people of Jerusalem slidden back by a perpetual backsliding? They hold fast deceit, they refuse to return.

I hearkened and heard, but they spake not aright: no man repented him of his wickedness, Saying, What have I done? every one turned to his course, as the horse rusheth into battle. Yea, the stork in the heaven knoweth her appointed times; and the turtle and the crane and the swallow observe the time of their coming; but my people know not the judgment of the LORD.

(Hosea 11:7) And my people are bent to backsliding from me: though they called them to the most High, none at all would exalt him.

There is no excuse for a believer who chooses to stay in the very act of rebellion, for Christ has made a way of escape for them. Sin has been put to death by the shedding of His blood on the cross. Continuing in sin without repentance is resurrecting that old man who has been crucified, for you have been delivered from sin and whom the son sets free is free indeed.

(1 Corinthians 10:13) There hath no temptation taken you but such as is common to man: but God is faithful, who will not suffer you

to be tempted above that ye are able; but will with the temptation also make a way to escape, that ye may be able to bear it.

(James 1:13-15) Let no man say when he is tempted, I am tempted of God: for God cannot be tempted with evil, neither tempteth he any man: But every man is tempted, when he is drawn away of his own lust, and enticed. Then when lust hath conceived, it bringeth forth sin: and sin, when it is finished, bringeth forth death. Do not err, my beloved brethren.

If this is your present state (**"backslider"** is one who was converted to Christianity but has reverted to their old habits and fallen into sin), for the pleasures *(Sin)* of this world have enticed you, drawing you on an ungodly pathway pursuing your own desire, then you have turned from your creator. You are living an unrepented life that has polluted your fellowship with God.

(1John 2:15-17) Love not the world, neither the things that are in the world. If any man love the world, the love of the father is not in him.

For all that is in the world, the lust of the flesh, and the lust of the eyes, and the pride of life, is not of the Father, but is of the world.

And the world passeth away, and the lust thereof: but he that doeth the will of God abideth for ever.

(Isaiah 59:1-2) Behold, the LORD's hand is not shortened that it cannot save, or his ear dull, that it cannot hear; but your iniquities have made a separation between you and your God, and your sins have hidden his face from you so that he does not hear.

U-turns will start the process of a 180° rotation to reverse the direction of the driver who was heading in the wrong way, veering from the original course. Stop, get your bearings, and turn around from your backsliding state, for God has never left you. It's you that has left Him. Use your headlights; put them on bright. See the U-turn neon signs. Repent, for God is a forgiving Father, waiting on you to make a turnaround—right back to his loving arms.

(1 John 1:9) If we confess our sins, he is faithful and just to forgive us our sins, and to cleanse us from all unrighteousness.

Every time you hear the word of God, from a born again believer, witnessing to you this is a sign activated and painted in bright red, the blood of Jesus has given you the victory **U-Turns are permitted**. Drivers now that you are headed toward your God ordained purpose stay focused, and go ahead and pump up the volume, listen to the gospel message through song and give your God the praise for all that he has done.

(Ephesians 5:19) Speaking to yourselves in psalms and hymns and spiritual songs, singing and making melody in your heart to the Lord;

Walk in the light! **(1John 1:5-6) This then is the message which we have heard of him, and declare unto you, that God is light, and in him is no darkness at all. If we say that we have fellowship with him, and walk in darkness, we lie, and do not the truth:**

Stay on the right path and plan of God for a successful life in Him, Your steps are order by Him, so walk, think and exemplify the very characteristics of Jesus Christ.

(1 Peter 2:21) **For even hereunto were ye called: because Christ also suffered for us, leaving us an example, that ye should follow his steps:** A Christian must keep on stepping! We must keep ourselves out of places that consists of entrapments and sin. *(1 Thessalonians 5:22)* **Abstain from all appearance of evil.**

Chapter 9

Narrow and Wide Gate!
(Right and Wrong Way)

(Matthew 7:13-14), Enter ye in at the strait gate; for wide is the gate, and broad is the way that leadeth to destruction, and many there be which go in thereat: Because strait is the gate, and narrow is the way which leadeth unto life, and few there be that find it.

"Jesus teaches about two pathways that one's choices conduct of life will lead them on."

1. Straight and Narrow—leads to life (The travelers or Christian's), path of the righteous.
2. Wide and Broad—leads to destruction (sinners, unbelievers in Jesus Christ), path of the wicked.

Humanity has been given the opportunity to choose which road to travel on Life's journey. These two pathways are not to be taken lightly; we must understand that each path has its own everlasting rewards.

"Straight and Narrow" The requirement for entrance is faith in Jesus Christ (Salvation)

The path of the righteous **(Psalm 23:3) He restoreth my soul: he leadeth me in the paths of righteousness for his name's sake.** The believer's born again life entails living according to the word of God. This narrow pathway is "tight but right"; living for Jesus comes with a price of denying yourself daily. **"If you can give it up, you can have it all."** Put your flesh in check. The Bible tells Christians to crucify the flesh (daily putting it to death against its own will and desire) and follow after Christ on this narrow pathway—but you are not traveling alone. **(Galatians 5:24) And they that are Christ's have crucified the flesh with the affections and lusts Wide and Broad Gate, pathway of the wicked** *"Any and everything goes!"*

Ancestral sin allotted humanity a spot on this 'out of order' pathway without any Boundaries; there is unlimited space for folly and debauchery. This path encourages mankind to "step right on up to do their own thing"—transgression of God's Law.

(1 John 3:4) Whosoever committeth sin transgresseth also the law: for sin is the transgression of the law.

"Carrying baggage"

When I think about traveling by air, and how strict airlines are about checking in baggage, I would try very hard not to over pack. I would find myself needing everything. Only going away for three days, I would pack like I was staying for two weeks. At curb-side assistant, the ticket agents would place my luggage on a scale, and there were times that it would be overweight. Too much stuff in my baggage, having to either remove some items or pay the hefty price for extra weight.

Sin is baggage that weighs a person's life down—disconnects them from the only true living God that can get rid of their heavy load. A person who loves worldly pleasures and is all about me, myself and I is blind and deaf to the truth of their own dilemma that brought about the unrighteous which impedes one's acceptance of the Gospel of Jesus Christ.

(Ephesians 4:18) Having the understanding darkened, being alienated from the life of God through the ignorance that is in them, because of the blindness of their heart.

Holding onto immorality and wickedness, not wanting to unload the excess baggage instead of Releasing it, thinking they are protecting their own valuables. Holding onto unforgiveness, bitterness, and anger's heavy burdens. God is not in their lives, leaving a void that no man or woman could ever fill.

- *(1).* Travelers of the wide gate will receive a reward: eternal death/ damnation.
- *(2).* Travelers of the narrow gate will receive a great reward: everlasting life.

You must receive Jesus Christ as your Lord and Savior, which is God's prerequisite in order to enter. Jesus said, "I am the gate *[to eternal life]*; whoever enters through me will be saved."

(John 10:9) **I am the door: by me if any man enter in, he shall be saved, and shall go in and out, and find pasture.**

Natural and Spiritual traveler!

In earlier chapters, I spoke about a man whose name was Saul (Paul), a traveler on the road to destruction. Let's look at him as a natural traveler: after he received spiritual sight (became born again), he was considered a spiritual traveler. As a spiritual traveler under inspiration of the Holy Spirit, he penned 13 epistles in the New Testament. When God changed Paul's life, He took him off the road of destruction and placed Him on the road of victory. *(Acts 9:8-9)* **And Saul arose from the earth; and when his eyes were opened, he saw no man: but they led him by the hand, and brought him into Damascus and he was three days without sight, and neither did eat nor drink.** God's love for all mankind includes the murderer *(killer)* of Christians. The power of the presence of Jesus knocked him off his course of action. He was pursuing Christians to kill them, because they were followers of Jesus. His plan of destruction was put to an end, and he himself became apprehended of the Lord Jesus the Christ. The scripture stated above shows that when Saul was heading in the wrong direction, grace and mercy were extended to him. Jesus, the light of the world, shined bright in his darkness.

Truth of the living word was manifested, for light always dispels darkness.

Trip stoppers! Travel on the wide gate!

I enjoy traveling, but one of my pet peeves is the trip stopper. A trip stopper is an obstacle that interrupts the flow of the excursion.

Throughout my life, I have spent a lot of time preparing for trips. Whenever my family and I are ready to head out the door, all kinds of things happen to delay us. Some examples are heading out my front door and the phone rings, having an unexpected guest knock at my door, or having to use the restroom.

Other examples I know many can relate to: misplaced cell phone, glasses, and keys, The devil, who is the enemy, comes to kill, steal, and destroy. He is a thief at work trying to stop Christians from God's assignments. **The thief cometh not, but for to steal, and to kill, and to destroy: I am come that they might have life, and that they might have it more abundantly.**

(John 10:10 KJV)

The trip stopper wants to prevent a person from traveling the right pathway, lurking around every corner, alleyway, and crevice, trying daily to stop someone from the only way to heaven by presenting false religion that pollutes lives with deception. Some have even denounced the one and only way to heaven, because they obeyed the trip stopper (the devil and his cohorts).

The pathway for the righteous is bright, full of light, and darkness is not permitted.

But the path of the just is as the shining sunlight, That shines ever brighter unto the perfect day. (Proverbs 4:18 KJV)

I praise the Lord for all the things he has done and continues to do in my life. I am so grateful that I am no longer bound, on a course of destruction. As a disciple of Jesus Christ, I have heavenly purpose: to achieve all that has been divinely planned for my life in the Kingdom of

God. His divine directive is the key for a Christian to have a successful journey.

Blessed is the man that walketh not in the counsel of the ungodly, nor standeth in the way of sinners, nor sitteth in the seat of the scornful. But his delight is in the law of the LORD; and in his law doth he meditate day and night. (Psalms 1:1-2 KJV)

"Spiritual Nourishment"

God has made His word available to the believer. It is life-sustaining nourishment that helps them to grow and live according to the Holy Bible. The Bible, in a natural sense, is like a smorgasbord for one's soul and mind. It is prepared to provide the student with everything they need to be equipped for service in the kingdom of God. There is no excuse for a child of God. To be malnourished is ignoring the need for a healthy appetite—it is not indulging daily in the Word of God.

An old saying comes to mind: "You are what you eat". I heard this saying quite often as I grew up. According to Ginger Software Phrase and Definition Origin & Examples, the first mention of the phrase "you are what you eat came" from the 1826 work *Physiologie du Goût ou Meditations de Gastronomie Transcendante*, in which French author Anthelme Brillat-Savarin wrote, "Tell me what you eat, and I will tell you what you are".

Metaphorically, the expression is to imply that what a person eats will affect their lives. To illustrate, if you were served a meal for dinner (fried chicken, baked macaroni and cheese, corn on the cob, and for dessert apple pie *à la mode*), and you waste no time in cleaning your plate, your stomach is full. You can feel your eyes getting low, and you're ready to take a nap. You consumed a meal with nourishment as your gain. Understand this: if it was not for God, there wouldn't have been any food on your table.

God has prepared a spiritual meal for his children that provides us everything we need (sustenance).

But he answered and said, it is written, Man shall not live by bread alone, but by every word that proceedeth out of the mouth of God. (Matthew 4:4 KJV)

A righteous believer must always proceed forward and detach from the ungodly, sinful desires of this world. One must walk in obedience according to the will of God. His children must be characterized by righteousness to become ambassadors for Christ. Ambassadors for Christ are those who inherit the promise of blessings and receive benefits that are given here on earth and in heaven.

The Way of the Wicked! Spiritually Dead

The Merriam-Webster dictionary defines ungodly as denying or disobeying God. For the ungodly do not know God, and want nothing to do with Him. They are driven by their own sinful desire. They are considered enemies of God, and their choice to forsake Him brings about death.

For the wages of sin is death; but the gift of God is eternal life through Jesus Christ our Lord. (Romans 6:23 KJV)

I was told growing up not to hang out with dead things, for they need to be buried *(an unsaved person is like the living dead)*. They will pollute your system and your life, if you let them, for they are inwardly rotten to the core, because of their sin nature. They need a spiritual transplant (becoming born again). Until that dead thing is delivered, it cannot be helped!

They have no spiritual life. The fall of Adam took us all to this state of being spiritually dead. I once operated in this 'out of order', wicked way, evil in thought and life full of sin. Many have pleasure in this pathway, but its true identity is one of deceit. Christian who marries someone outside of their faith is going against biblical scripture. That kind of relationship is considered unequally yoked—when they decide to attach themselves to someone in any form or fashion to those who love not their God or want to receive Him into their hearts.

(2 Corinthians 6:14) **Be ye not unequally yoked together with unbelievers: for what fellowship hath righteousness with unrighteousness? And what communion hath light with darkness? Good and evil don't mix!**

If you are connected to someone who is not connected to God, you are operating opposite of His plan for your life. What he said not to do, you did it anyway. Don't get upset when all hell breaks loose. When you consciously attach yourself to an ungodly person who wants nothing to do with your Jesus, you can expect problems.

(1 Corinthians 15:34) **Awake to righteousness, and sin not; for some have not the knowledge of God: I speak this to your shame.**

(Psalms 1:4-6) **The ungodly are not so: but are like the chaff which the wind drives away. Therefore the ungodly shall not stand in the judgment, nor sinners in the congregation of the righteous, For _the_**

<u>**Lord knows the way of the righteous**</u>, **But the way of the ungodly shall perish.**

When I was a young girl, there was a group of teenagers who always started trouble with me *(bullies)*. There wasn't a motive for them harassing me. They were just mean-spirited individuals. Some of my peers were afraid of these hooligans. So, instead of standing up to them, I became a part of their shenanigans. We must not associate with people who are angry, bitter, and disrespectful to others and don't desire to change. A seed was planted when I was being bullied. I also found myself bullying others. I finally made a decision not to continue down the path of bullying. I knew this was not who I wanted to be, so I separated myself from the bullies. A blessed person loves God and delights in doing his will. He or she is found meditating day and night on the word of God. This analogy of a tree regarding blessed people encouraged my heart:

(Palms 1:3) And shall be like a tree planted by the rivers of water, that brings forth his fruit in his season; his leaf also shall not wither; And whatsoever he doeth shall prosper.

The righteous are led by the Holy Spirit, so don't grieve or quench him by doing your own thing, for the just shall live by faith. It is the only one way for those who belong to God, for he says we are to be Holy as he is Holy. We are never alone.

Wake up call! Get off the wide path!

I had a nephew who was in his twenties when he put a gun to his head and committed suicide. His life was suddenly gone. He shot himself in the presence of his only sister. He went to see her to say goodbye.

Unfortunately, I did not get a chance to see my nephew on the day of his demise. In hindsight, my brother told me that my nephew wanted to visit me, but this did not occur. Something serious happened to this young man. He was very discontent with life and got involved in all types of bad decisions. His death by his own hands devastated the entire family, his friends, and shocked the entire community. It was the talk of the neighborhood for quite some time. This was truly unexpected. The last conversation that I had with him was mainly about hurts and pain. This was an opportunity to witness about God and being a part of His royal family. At the time, before his passing, he was in a gang. I strongly believe the bond he had to this particular group of people brought chaos into his life. He once told me that he could never leave the gang. He called them family. This was the last encounter I had with this handsome dreamer *(aka my nephew)*. I can recall receiving the disturbing news. At that time, I was living with my sister-in-law. When she handed me the telephone, she said, "Do not get upset" *(she didn't know what else to say)*. After hearing the news, I threw the phone against the wall. I couldn't believe what I heard.

This was a wakeup call! There are several young people who are hurting and suffering who really need guidance today. They need wise counsel, and those in their lives who love God. Who will listen to them, regardless of how crazy they sound. I was asked by the family if I would preside over the funeral, since I was a licensed/ordained minister. Unaware at this time these words were a prophetic "wakeup call" by separating my emotional grief aside and switching into prayer mode, I asked God to give me His comforting words to allow me to minister to those in distress during this time of bereavement. According to **Revelation 21:4 KJV: "And God shall wipe away all tears from their eyes; and there**

shall be no more death, neither sorrow, nor crying, neither shall there be any more pain: for the former things are passed away."

Earth has no sorrows that heaven can't heal!

While preparing the eulogy in prayer, I asked God what would He have me say to those attending my nephew's funeral. The message was that it's a wakeup call! This was by far one of the hardest, most difficult moments in my life. Also, it was the first funeral I ever presided over. Many high emotions—I felt many family and friends were hurting, grieving, angry, and confused at this trying time.

Many friends who loved Jason had a question: why did he take his own life, and what went wrong? As I attempted to answer them, I sought guidance from the Holy Spirit. The funeral home was packed with friends and family; there was barely any room to stand. So many young adults were shaken by his death. God had a word for them of endearment, tender affection, and the truth of salvation. Many present were on the wide path of destruction. Mankind does not know when its earthly journey will come to an end. Tomorrow is not promised to anyone—nor today for that matter. This is a wakeup call for everyone that we all will die. One should take into consideration that life is precious. They should view any funeral service as their own, since it is inevitable that we all must go through this experience called death, but as long as there is breath in your body, and you're above ground and not beneath it, there is an opportunity to accept God's love and forgiveness. This is made possible by His only Son Jesus, who is the way of salvation. A funeral is for the dead (a home-going service is for the Christians)—a time of sorrow and pain where we reflect on the deceased. With that in mind, don't procrastinate, because if you don't prepare for eternity, there's no second chance once you die. Wake up!

"Total Wreck"

CHAPTER 10

Yes! Jesus Is The Only Way! To Heaven!

"Jesus Is the Way, the Truth, and the Life"

Jesus saith unto him, I am the way, the truth, and the life: no man cometh unto the Father, but by me. (John 14:4 KJV) Jesus told his disciples that he was leaving them and returning back to his father's house in glory *(Heaven)*. He said that one day they would be with him. **Simon Peter said unto him, Lord, whither goest thou? Jesus answered him, whither I go, thou canst not follow me now; but thou shalt follow me afterwards.(John 13:36 KJV)**

Jesus, the Son of God, is the only answer for people who want to be saved and set free. He offers all eternal life, if they choose to receive his Redeeming Love and enter into the only way open.

Then said Jesus unto them again, Verily, verily, I say unto you, I am the door of the sheep.

All that ever came before me are thieves and robbers: but the sheep did not hear them.

I am the door; by me if any man enter in, he shall be saved, and shall go in and out, and find pasture. (John 10:7-9)

The blood of Jesus that was shed is the foundation of redemption for mankind. God has given a priceless, life-sustaining source for transforming lives. **In him was life, and the life was the light of men. (John 1:4 KJV)**

No other way to God was made! Jesus was chosen by God to be the way out of no way! He is the only savior of the world. Not believing and receiving Jesus will cost a person everything. It is not over when one meets their earthly demise. Those who don't believe that there's a place called heaven will be in for a rude awakening when they find out that the way they chose did not provide access to God for them.

Neither is there salvation in any other: for there is none other name under heaven given among men, whereby we must be saved. (Acts 4:12 KJV)

Those who worship an idol of some sort, be it a statute of a man or animal, etc. (false gods), do not know that they are truly serving the fallen angel—the enemy of all mankind (Satan). His job is to keep one from the truth that Yes! Jesus is the only way to God. He's been on this mission for a very long time, and he will not stop. Presenting lies is just what he does; the truth is not in him.

Christianity is founded on the principles and teachings of Jesus Christ, the Son of God. A person who is a true Christian is one who believes in Jesus Christ as their personal Savior. If you are one who believes that you can use any other name, you are dismissing the only way that God has provided for humanity. Nothing or no one except Jesus is going to get you into heaven.

Think about the following questions:

1. Are you really sure about your destiny and on the right pathway?
2. What if you are wrong about the way to the only true God?
3. Do you want to miss out on such a great blessing to be with God forever in heaven?
4. Do you want to ask Jesus to save you and come into your heart—making sure you are on the right pathway?

Heaven is reserved for those who are redeemed by the blood of the Lamb. Jesus came to the earth as a lamb to be slaughtered for our sins. **He was oppressed, and he was afflicted, yet he opened not his mouth: he is brought as a lamb to the slaughter. (Isaiah 53:7)**

A person who has accepted God's Son *(Jesus)* as their only way out of guilt and condemnation is the recipient of promises and privileges now and hereafter. They have a dwelling place waiting for them in *Heaven*, where there is no more pain, suffering, crying, sickness, loneliness, or death. It's contentment, peace, and joy in the Holy Spirit—praising and worshipping our heavenly Father for all eternity *(Hallelujah)*.

And God shall wipe away all tears from their eyes; and there shall be no more death, neither sorrow, nor crying, neither shall there be

any more pain: for the former things are passed away. (Revelation 21:4)

There is heavenly documentation which validates your status of a heavenly registry *(roll call or ledger)* for all born again residents (those who met the required prerequisite for entrance). When someone accepts Jesus as their Lord and Savior, they become a child of God, and their name is written in heaven. *(Luke 10:20)* **. . . because your names are written in heaven.**

"Jesus was born in Bethlehem"

When the announcement of Jesus' prophetic birth was proclaimed, wise men came asking King Herod where this "newborn king" was. *(Matthew 2:2)* **Saying, Where is he that is born King of the Jews? For we have seen his star in the east: and are come to worship him.**

These wise men were on a journey to find the "King of the Jews" and to celebrate his arrival by presenting gifts and worshipping Him. The wise men were unaware of the jealousy the King experienced after he heard the announcement. **When Herod the king had heard these things, he was troubled, and all Jerusalem with him. (Matthew 2:3)**

His response was birthed from a murderous intent of anger and fear. He wanted to kill the Messiah at birth. This was an innocent child. The ungodly King was so upset that he demanded his chief priests and scribes tell him where Christ was going to be born (he had an evil mindset). He inquired whether he would be born in Bethlehem of Judaea.

The birth of Jesus is a story that one can only imagine. Throughout historical times, and even today, when the name Jesus is mentioned, some people get very upset. They want to kill *(execute)* Christ anew. They removed prayer out of the public schools and replacing it with nothing. They replaced the celebration of Christ's birth with the focus on a fat, old man in a red and white suit called Santa Claus ("Good Ol' Saint Nick").

Religions which believe they are following something or someone other than Jesus have been duped and misguided for centuries. When other forms of spiritualism are discussed, there isn't an uproar. However, when the name of Jesus is mentioned, many get offended. This should set off an alarm and a red flag should arise in one's mind to investigate thoroughly. Seeking the truth should be our field work. It is so apparent that evil forces have been assigned to come up against the only way for man to enter into the Kingdom of heaven. So, I ask once again, are you really sure you have access to heaven's entry gate? If you can honestly say, "I'm not sure," I then implore you to seek God while you still have breath in your body.

A siren should sound off inside of your heart as the light goes on, revealing truth to your mind and soul. Please, pay close attention to the news reports, wars, violence, senseless crimes, gender bias, inequality, starvation, and earthquakes in diverse places. There is "nothing new under the sun." Wars between good and evil have been present since the beginning of time. There is a spiritual battle between God and Lucifer. Observe the big picture; it's all because of the infiltrator (the devil) trying anything and everything to stop you from being reconciled back to God. *"YES! JESUS IS THE ONLY WAY!" (In no other name but the name of Jesus)* through which men might be saved.

Neither is there salvation in any other: for there is none other name under heaven given among men, whereby we must be saved. (Acts 4:12 KJV)

That at the name of Jesus every knee should bow, of things in heaven, and things in earth, and things under the earth; And that every tongue should confess that Jesus Christ is Lord, to the glory of God the Father. (Philippians 2:10-11)

For now we are able to expose the lies of the enemy by the teaching and preaching the gospel of Jesus Christ. Jesus testified and declared "that he is the only way the truth and the life, and no man comes to the Father but by him." **(John 14: 6)**

I thank God I received a cancellation of my ticket to the destination called hell. I can't even imagine not having God as my heavenly Father, having him in my life, or being in heaven. I thank Jesus for loving me and saving my life from eternal damnation. He has given me a new destination, and on this journey I have peace and eternal life. Jesus spoke about his departure publicly and privately to his disciples; He emphatically told them that he was going to his Father's house. This stirred up a question in the mind of His disciples. They wanted to know where He was going.

(John 13:36) Simon Peter said unto him, Lord, whither goest thou? Jesus answered him, Whither I go, thou canst not follow me now; but thou shalt follow me afterwards.

Questions that are asked today should be answered with truth and love. It's time to be real and not beat around the bush. **(John 14:5) Thomas saith unto him, Lord, we know not whither thou goest; and how can we**

know the way? Thomas had the very same question that many have today: how can we know the way?

My active readers, my question to you is this: are you ready to receive the absolute answers?

Hear the words of Jesus responding to Thomas' question. **Jesus saith unto him, "I am the way, the truth, and the life: no man cometh unto the Father, but by me".**

(John 14:2-3) **In my Father's house are many mansions: if it were not so, I would have told you. I go to prepare a place for you. And if I go and prepare a place for you, I will come again, and receive you unto myself; that where I am, there ye may be also.**

Jesus is the only answer! There is no other way one can get you into heaven; it is only by the precious blood of the Savior. Don't be fooled or tricked and end up finding out that you were severely wrong and have to face a sign which reads "no entry"! You blew it! You had a chance but denied the only way to God: Jesus. He is our only lifeline and source of liberty from sin.

No one was able to pay such a hefty price. Jesus was tortured unmercifully and suffered the unimaginable and horrendous death of crucifixion.

Jesus predicts His Death: **And Jesus going up to Jerusalem took the twelve disciples apart in the way, and said unto them, Behold, we go up to Jerusalem: and the Son of man shall be betrayed unto the chief priests and unto the scribes, and they shall condemn him to death, And shall deliver him to the Gentiles to mock, and to scourge, and to crucify him: and the third day he shall rise again.** (Matthew 20:17-19)

Jesus went through the pain and suffering so mankind could be afforded a great opportunity to repent from their sins, receive Him as Lord and Savior, and live with him for all eternity. He suffered and died, and his resurrection gave us assurance of entrance into the Kingdom of God. When a person receives Jesus as their Lord and Savior, they cross over from death to life. **Verily, verily, I say unto you, He that heareth my word, and believeth on him that sent me, hath everlasting life, and shall not come into condemnation; but is passed from death unto life. (John 5:24)**

Because Jesus rose from the dead, we have a blessed assurance that we, too, also shall be raised.

But if the Spirit of him that raised Jesus from the dead dwell in you, he that raised up Christ from the dead shall also quicken your mortal bodies by his Spirit that dwelleth in you. (Romans 8:11) We will rise "like getting up in the morning", leaving our grave clothes behind, never to return to them—having instead a glorified body.

For this corruptible must put on incorruption, and this mortal must put on immortality. So when this corruptible shall have put on incorruption, and this mortal shall have put on immortality, then shall be brought to pass the saying that is written, Death is swallowed up in victory. O death, where is thy sting? O grave, where is thy victory? (1 Corinthians 15:53-55) But thanks be to God, which giveth us the victory through our Lord Jesus Christ. (1 Corinthians 15:57)

Christ knew no sin but bore our sins in His own body on a tree (cross). He died and was buried on good Friday in a tomb borrowed from a man named Joseph of Arimathea. He rose up from the grave early Sunday morning. The grave could not hold him—nor could the tomb that was borrowed. The tomb was rented for the weekend only! He alone is our way maker! Through His death and resurrection, he reconciled fallen humanity back to God! He is the bridge and the advocate for the world.

Reconciliation! by the way maker Jesus Christ the blessed Savior of the world.

The only way for mankind to be reconciled to God is through Jesus! He was crucified at a place that is called in Hebrew Golgotha's Hill (Calvary). **And as they came out, they found a man of Cyrene, Simon by name: him they compelled to bear his cross. And when they were come unto a place called Golgotha, that is to say, a place of a skull, (Matthew 27:32-33);** *[Reference verses, Mark 15:22; John 19:17]*

His death on the cross was prophesied in the Old Testament Book of Isaiah *(53:4-6)*

Surely he hath borne our griefs, and carried our sorrows: yet we did esteem him stricken, smitten of God, and afflicted; but he was wounded for our transgressions, he was bruised for our iniquities: the chastisement of our peace was upon him; and with his stripes we are healed.

Jesus, our catalyst, made atonement by His sacrificial death that propitiated reconciliation for humanity. His blood sacrificed on this cross of anguish provided the only access to heaven.

(Galatians 3:13) **Christ hath redeemed us from the curse for us: of the law, being made a curse for us: for it is written, Cursed is everyone that hangeth on a tree.**

He reconciled us back to God. ***"YES JESUS IS THE ONLY WAY"!*** Redemption by Christ through shed blood. *(Ephesians 1:7)* **In whom we have redemption through his blood, the forgiveness of sins, according to the riches of his grace;**

Humanity—we were and still are a people today in need of a Savior!

Wherefore remember, that ye being in time past Gentiles in the flesh, who are called Uncircumcision by that which is called the Circumcision in the flesh made by hands; That at that time ye were without Christ, being aliens from the commonwealth of Israel, and strangers from the covenants of promise, having no hope, and without God in the world: But now in Christ Jesus ye who sometimes were far off are made nigh by the blood of Christ. (Ephesians 2:11-13)

I remember living without Christ. I was so empty! I felt unfulfilled and searched for what I thought would make me happy and complete. I thought that living the American dream was all I needed: being married, having a child, and pursuing my dream job *(career)* to become a model. An empty feeling was always present. I was never truly content in what I tried to achieve.

Without Christ, I was in the category of people the Bible identifies as **aliens**: illegal strangers of the covenant of God, His promises, and no spiritual inheritance. A person without Christ is in need of adoption, in order to have eternal life. When you are adopted into the family of God, you become part of a royal priesthood.

For ye have not received the spirit of bondage again to fear; but ye have received the Spirit of adoption, whereby we cry, Abba, Father. (Romans 8:15)

Adoption gives one access to the Kingdom of God, becoming part of a family divinely connected—recipient of a Godly inheritance, having been given a new divine nature in him.

Therefore if any man be in Christ, he is a new creature: old things are passed away; behold, all things are become new. (2 Corinthians 5:17)

Christians are joint heirs with Christ, having the right to receive this title of sons of God.

For as many as are led by the Spirit of God, they are the sons of God. (Romans 8:14)

(Romans 8:17) And if children, then heirs; heirs of God, and joint-heirs with Christ; if so be that we suffer with him, that we may be also glorified together.

The Redeemer and Savior of the world paid it all, cleansing mankind's sins with his own blood on the cross! We are justified freely by his grace through the redemption that is in Christ Jesus, whom God hath set forth to be a propitiation through faith in his blood, to declare unto us his righteousness for the remission of sins that are past, all through the forbearance of God.

"I Almost Missed Heaven"

CHAPTER 11

Highway to Hell! What In Hell Do You Want?

One day, I was asked to preach at a church. My assignment from God was a message with a question: "What in Hell do you want?" This message had a resounding answer, emphatic to the hearers response: "there is nothing in hell I want!" I once was on that very path of doom— on a highway to hell with my foot on the gas pedal. My initial thought was that hell is here on earth, but there is an eternal destination for all who were born in sin and shaped in iniquity. For one who makes their bed in hell **(Hell-Bent)**, there is no return. Their boarding pass or ticket is stamped "sin", and on the other side its states "Destination: Hell"! This is an ungodly, dreadful place, where many have chosen to reside, since they have refused to accept Jesus Christ as Lord and Savior! This rejection will drive them to a forbidden place called Hell. *(eternal torment of fire)* **And the devil that deceived them was cast**

into the lake of fire and brimstone, where the beast and the false prophet are, and shall be tormented day and night for ever and ever. (Rev 20:10) Hell was made for Satan and the fallen angels, but people have chosen to go to this dreadful place. People have chosen all kinds of false gods, have joined cults, and have polluted their minds with a pack of lies. They will find themselves destined for hellfire. Counterfeiters or pretenders say that they believe in God, but they deny Jesus Christ as the only way to make it into heaven. You have to get a visual of the kind of people that are going to be in hell—some of those who have good intentions. Those people say, "I never hurt anyone, I feed the poor, I don't lie, steal, or even drink alcohol or take drugs. I occasionally visit the sick and those who are incarcerated, and I have done my civic duties." These are all good intentions, but they cannot get you into heaven!

They're occasionally attending church, making confession to a priest of the sins one has committed, paying tithes and offering, and even giving a little more on special occasions. Also included in the hell community are murders, people who practice sexual perversion, prejudiced people, drug dealers and users, all kinds of families in general and professionally, the rich and poor *("Status quo")*. There is no discrimination at all in a place of eternal anguish and separation from God. All because of unbelief and doubt, when all one has to do is to receive Jesus into their heart and be saved. While there is still breath in your body, there is still a chance of hope for you to accept the only way that God has prepared through His Son Jesus Christ.

To the people who have said that they believe in Jesus but there is no inner change, let me ask you this question: did you ask Jesus to save you, to come into your heart? First, one must acknowledge that they are a sinner in need of the only Savior. When one receives this gift of Salvation, it is like no other. It is a life-altering, refreshing, reviving, and forever changed experience. The very horrors of hell have been canceled for you, travelers! Be encouraged, knowing that when you die *(sleep)*, you have prepared yourself for heaven. **We are confident, I say, and willing rather to be absent from the body, and to be present with the Lord. (2 Corinthians 5:8)**

It is a blessing to have received the love of God and to be able to share with others (family, friends, and strangers). Sometimes being able to witness His love in action in their lives brings joy to my heart.

"The Holman Bible Dictionary" defines Hell as the abode of the dead. It is an Anglo-Saxon word used to translate one Hebrew word and three Greek words in the King James Version of the Old and New Testaments. The Hebrew word for "hell" is is Sheol. The three Greek words often translated as "hell" are Hades, Gehenna, and Tartaroo.

In *Luke 16:19-31*, Jesus speaks in a parable about an unnamed man who is only identified as a certain rich man; his material gain and wealth is noted. A description of his attire was given, as well. This man had on expensive clothing, wearing purple garments (this color represents royalty) and fine linen, and he feasted sumptuously every day. There was no shame to his game, lavishly living it up. Jesus explained so clearly: certainly there are eternal consequences when wealth is your god. This man was unjust to the poor; he was very narcissistic. His self-indulgence and selfish nature were evident. As the story continues, a man named Lazarus, whose name means "one whom God helps," is described as a beggar. He was a destitute man, and he laid outside the rich man's gate daily, hoping that he would receive any amount of food, be it crumbs that might fall from the wealthy man's table. Lazarus' physical condition was poor health, afflicted, full of sores, and covered with ulcers and boils on his body. The only compassion given was from a pack of dogs: they licked Lazarus' sores. One day, both men died; one was pictured as going to Hades. The word Hades is equivalent to the Hebrew Sheol, referring to the realm of the dead immediately after death, before final judgment. Hades is described as having parts. **"The other was in Abraham's bosom"**, a place of honor and fellowship, and this was the destination of Lazarus. He was carried by angels, transported to a place of heavenly bliss—paradise. Doesn't this sound wonderful! Wow! Paradise and heaven!

("☹ Hell sounds unbearably hot")

A place were man will suffer agony, anguish, torture, and be without God is no place for anyone. *(Luke 13:28)* **There shall be weeping and gnashing of teeth . . . the bible says!**

These words are also used to identify this awful place called Hell! "The lake of fire" or second death. Unbelievers must be warned before it's too late for them, just like it was too late for this rich man. He had some nerve, wanting Lazarus to give him water!

And in hell he lifted up his eyes, being in torments: and seeth Abraham afar off, and Lazarus in his bosom: And he cried and said: Father Abraham, have mercy on me: and send Lazarus that he may dip the tip of his finger in water, and cool my tongue: for I am tormented in this flame. (Luke 16:23-24)

The bible says that Abraham spoke to the rich man who was experiencing great torment.

But Abraham said, "Son, remember that thou in thy lifetime received thy good things: and likewise Lazarus evil things but now he is comforted: and thou art tormented." *(Luke 16:25)*

The rich man wanted water, but his request could never be granted; there was a huge gulf between them. **And besides all this, between us and you there is a great gulf fixed: so that they which would pass from hence to you cannot; neither can they pass to us, that would come from thence. (Luke 16:26)**

He could not get this request, so he made another request, now understanding that this hell is real. He did not want his family members who were headed on this same pathway to come to this place of no escape. **Then he said, I pray thee Therefore, father, that thou wouldest send him to my father's house: For I have five brethren; that he may testify unto them, lest they also come into this place of torment. Abraham saith unto him, They have Moses and the prophets; let them hear them. And he said, Nay, father Abraham: but if one went unto them from the dead, they will repent. (Luke 16:27-30)**

This man's discussion with Abraham is quite revealing, because Abraham left the earth a long time before this man's demise. We then learn from this text that interaction (verbal communication) after one's earthly demise happens. However, he fails to validate his point that if Lazarus, who also died, goes and tells his family, they will believe him. Abraham's answer alludes to this very fact, that Moses and the Prophets foretold of the coming of Christ, which is the gospel (The death, burial, and resurrection of the Son of God).

And he said unto him, If they hear not Moses and the prophets, neither will they be persuaded, though one rose from the dead. (Luke 16:31)

Jesus' redemptive death "for our sins" allowed mankind a chance to be redeemed and exit the highway to hell! This is the only possible way to heaven for the living who still have breath in their body. This is a very important personal decision to make, so you better take it seriously. When one leaves this earth, that's all she wrote! There is no second chance after death!

The bible says, **And as it is appointed unto men once to die, but after this the judgment. (Hebrews 9:27)**

There are some people in our society who are making plans or preparations for their demise, so that the surviving family won't have to worry about handling funeral arrangements.

They prepare everything, so that the family knows where the "last will and testament" is located, so they can adhere to all of your wishes concerning your belongings and assets to be assigned to your loved ones. The main point here: are you really sure of your final resting place? Are you heaven-bound? While you were alive and had breath in your body, did you accept Jesus Christ as Lord and Savior? or are you going to spend eternity in hell?

I say to you: there is nothing in Hell I want! Having experienced menopause for about 10 years, hot flashes ain't no joke! The rich man in the bible felt water would help him; he was hot. I tried all kinds of things for hot flashes—I am just saying, Hell is not a place for me! The main reason I would not want that place to be my abode is knowing that I would be eternally separated from God.

(No Thanks!)

CHAPTER 12

Salvation is for you!

When a person has accepted this life-changing decision of liberation, they are delivered from bondage and made whole. They are no longer bound to or a slave to sin but have been reconciled to God through Jesus' life, death, and resurrection. Jesus showed us the way to salvation, instructing us how to live this Christian life once we received him as our Lord and Savior.

Today is your golden opportunity, right now, to receive salvation and deliverance from the penalty and power of sin. I am speaking to all who have ears to hear and are willing to receive Jesus as Lord and Savior and receive the Holy Spirit. It is not by coincidence that you are reading this book. Some might be thinking, "Hey, I am the one who bought this book." Yes, this is true (may God richly bless you), but my belief is that everything is planned and orchestrated by God for you to receive this testimonial manuscript. Emphatically, Jesus truly loves you, and he wants you to be reconciled unto him! Who is your source of salvation? I want you to know if you think you chose Him, No! It was that God has chosen you! You need to believe and receive.

But we are bound to give thanks always to God for you, brethren beloved of the Lord, because God hath from the beginning chosen you to salvation through sanctification of the Spirit and belief of the truth: (2Thessalonians 2:13)

Christ Alone!

This is a faithful saying, and worthy of all acceptation, that Christ Jesus came into the world to save sinners; of whom I am chief. (1 Timothy 1:15)

Many years ago, I remember what someone told me when they came to visit me in the hospital. They spoke about the car accident that I was in—how I was propelled several feet from the vehicle and sprawled out on the ground. Parts of the car wreckage were on top of my body. I was crying hysterically and was in excruciating pain. Someone said that I spoke the words, "Please don't leave me" in Spanish. This was shocking, because I didn't speak Spanish. Only a few profane words, along with some everyday words, like water *(agua)*, hot *(caliente)*, cold *(frio)*, and come here *(ven aqui)*. This person was also in the accident. Hearing the news of what had happened to me while sitting in my hospital bed put me in a state of awe. I looked at him, and my very thoughts were, "Yeah, right!" My response was, "I don't know how to say 'Please don't leave me' in Spanish" *(Por favor, no me dejes)*.

At that particular time in my life, salvation was far from me. I was not willing to accept this Awesome, almighty God, even though death was knocking at the door. I was "livin la vida loca" and on my way to a burning hell and being totally separated from God. My physical injuries consisted of a broken neck, broken hip, broken arm, leg broken in four places, also a pelvic fracture and a broken tooth. I obtained all of this in this horrific accident that changed my daily life. I am constantly reminded of that night, and it is burned in my heart, due to my physical ailments. I was at a crossroads, having to choose which path to take. The options were continuing on the path of destruction or the path of construction. Several years later, I understand now that God has given me the utterance of speaking in another language (Spanish). I believe that this would be a future sign for me after I accepted Jesus as my Lord and Savior. I was not speaking unto man, but unto God, even though others heard me speaking in their own language.

Now when this was noised abroad, the multitude came together, and were confounded because that every man heard them speak in his own language. (Acts 2:6)

The words "Please don't leave me" are profound cries of sorrow and confession. I truly thank you, Jesus, for saving me. My life was spared that very night. God's grace and mercy came into my broken life right at the nick of time. Undeserving of this grace that is unconditional, His love gave me a second chance. **"Christ alone"** has provided salvation, for anyone that places their faith in Him will be delivered from sins.

Nor is there salvation in any other, for there is no other name under heaven given among men by which we must be saved. (Acts 4:12)

"Being religious doesn't mean you received salvation!"

One who attends church service on Sunday or Saturday is not necessarily saved. Maybe you don't attend services every week. Perhaps you are content in staying home and watching your favorite television evangelist, sowing seeds into various ministries, feeding the poor, or visiting the sick and incarcerated, which is commendable. The bible says, **"For what shall it profit a man, if he shall gain the whole world, and lose his own soul?"** *(Mark 8:36).*

No one can obtain salvation through purchasing it or by meritorious deeds of kindness or moral goodness. These acts of religiosity without genuine faith in God are disobedient to the prerequisites to salvation.

Hereby know ye the Spirit of God: Every spirit that confesseth that Jesus Christ is come in the flesh is of God: (1John 4:2)

"For those who will receive salvation," there are two important factors:

Key # 1—Jesus is the only way, providing salvation for those who believe in him; this is a Christian's proclamation, for true confession leads to repentance.

Key # 2 – An undeniable fact: Jesus died and arose from the grave! You must believe the gospel message! **But these are written, that ye might believe that Jesus is the Christ, the Son of God; and that believing ye might have life through his name. (John 20:31)**

It's your Choice!

And if it seems evil unto you to serve the LORD, choose you this day whom ye will serve; whether the gods which your fathers served that were on the other side of the flood, or the gods of the Amorites,

in whose land ye dwell: but as for me and my house, we will serve the LORD. (Joshua 24:15)

I truly believe that everybody wants to go to heaven, but some are not willing to do the necessary requirements for entry. In this world, there are so many different kinds of religions *[thanks in part to our constitution; freedom of religion]*, which one is the real deal? This concept has confused many from receiving the gospel message. God is calling us to a relationship and family, not a shenanigan / traditional religion of discord and discontent. This opportunity of adoption into God's royal family is afforded to all those who are willing to accept the requirements of being in His family.

Having predestinated us unto the adoption of children by Jesus Christ to himself, according to the good pleasure of his will, (Ephesians 1:5)

It's very important to note that it's your choice where you will spend eternity. God gave us this very choice by sending His only-begotten Son, who came down from heaven in the flesh and dwelt with man. God's love for mankind had no restriction, giving us a free will to choose, since he chose you. **I speak not of you all: I know whom I have chosen . . . (John 13:18)**

Whosoever denieth the Son, the same hath not the Father: *[but] he that acknowledgeth the Son hath the Father also. (1 John 2:23)*

Biblical truths echo emphatically—resounding jewels of sacredness concerning Jesus as the only way to the Father. **That all men should honor the Son, even as they honor the father. He that honors not the Son honors not the Father which hath sent him. (John 2:23)**

I made my choice! By believing and receiving the truth of the Gospel of Jesus Christ, now I am heaven bound. God does not want anyone to choose wrong.

(2 Peter 3:9) . . . not willing that any should perish, but that all should come to repentance.

Without Christ, we are in a lost, unconnected state and must be reconciled back to him. If a person refuses to change, not surrendering their lives to the one that gave them life, this is a sad state of affairs. When someone comes to you, evangelizing the gospel of Jesus Christ, this is an opportunity that has been granted to you from God. Your decision time has come; don't throw away that opportunity to make the greatest choice you will ever make! God took the initiative by sending His Son-to die in our stead. His longsuffering and patient dispensation will not last always. Time is running out! So, please make the right decision for your life, before it's too late! Don't procrastinate or dwell in a state of being indecisive!

CHAPTER 13

God is a keeper!

God promises to keep the believer in perfect peace. This is an "if . . . then" principle [**if you do this, then God will do His part**]. "If" their mind stays on Him. **Thou wilt keep him in perfect peace, whose mind is stayed on thee: because he trusts in thee. (Isaiah 26:3)**

A keeper is one who guards, protects, or cares for something. God is our (Shepherd) Keeper, guarding and protecting his children. **The LORD is thy keeper: the LORD is thy shade upon thy right hand. (Psalm 121:5)**

Sheep are used throughout the Bible symbolically, referring to the people of God. A shepherd's primary responsibility is the safety and well-being of their flock. He will lead his sheep to graze in the field, keeping a watchful eye out on them, protecting them from predators or anything that can hurt them.

THE LORD is my shepherd; I shall not want. He makes me to lie down in green pastures: he leads me beside the still waters. He restores my soul: he leads me in the paths of righteousness for his name's sake. (Psalm 23:1)

God makes sure we have our provisions, always caring for his children; no one can do you like he can. I am reminded of times when money was scarce, not knowing where my next dollar was coming from. One day, God spoke to me. I heard a still, small voice, saying "crochet around metal."

Then I had a brain storm—a witty idea I gave birth to: creating crochet outfits in a metal shape of a person as candle holders, figurines, and creating many others things, selling them to meet my needs.

But my God shall supply all your need according to his riches in glory by Christ Jesus. (Philippians 4:19)

After the bad car accident I was in, my injuries had a cause and effect scenario, but I have personally experienced God as my keeper! In 1988, the doctors placed a rod in my hip, and my right leg was a half an inch shorter (which made me limp and need shoe lifts). The cost of a heel was $12 a shoe; this definitely ended my high heels days *(sob!)*. The stilettoes many are wearing today are very nice and beautiful, but I'll never be able to wear them, but that's okay, because I can still walk!

Thank you, Jesus! So, let me go on—I just had a shoe moment! Ladies, some of you know what I am talking about! Also my brothers who like their Stacey Adams can identify as well—just have to have that special pair.

I had experienced different kinds of physical pain for years before purchasing my shoe lifts, and not having them caused abdominal pain. No matter how I suffered in this body, I knew that God said He would "never leave me nor forsake me." Returning back into the workforce, after 12 years of convalescing from the car accident in 1988, I endured many challenges with prolonged sitting and standing. My determination to push past all the obstacles and trust God to strengthen me, keeping my mind on Him, has kept me in perfect peace!

"Stormy Situations"

When you are enduring a storm in your life, there are three main power points to remember:

1. Storms will come! They are inevitable; natural storms consist of disturbance of weather, of wind accompanied by rain or lighting, etc.
2. Your reactions are very important! (No knee-jerk reaction)
3. Know the Captain of your situations! (And if you don't, find out!)

Prior to Jesus entering the ship with his disciples, he was tired from the daily activities of prayer and ministering to the people. He went to the back of the ship and found a place to rest. As they were on their journey, all of a sudden there arose a storm that rocked the boat from side to side as the insurmountable storm increased! Can you just imagine the waves of the sea crashing inside of the boat? Jesus came to the rescue of His disciples in a storm situation, and He rebuked the wind and spoke to the sea, giving it a directive: "Peace, be still."

And he arose, and rebuked the wind and said unto the sea, Peace, be still. And the wind ceased, and there was a great calm. (Mark 4:39)

The reaction of the disciples was to panic and be afraid *(being trained fishermen, this storm was unusual in nature)*, as they went and woke Jesus **And he was in the hinder part of the ship, asleep on a pillow: and they awake him, and say unto him, Master, carest thou not that we perish? (Mark 4:38)**

The disciples barely knew who the captain was, yet they did inquire of His assistance. Jesus, who is the captain, arose from slumber, rebuked the winds and waves, and said, "Peace, be still!" Nature became obedient, knowing who their *(Creator)* and captain is!

The application we take from this story of a stormy situation for today is that we are to always activate our faith. We should not allow fear to cripple our faith! We don't always have control over our circumstances, but we must trust and depend on almighty God in the midst of everything that comes our way, causing us to be shaken and stirred up – no matter what happens! God will always protect his children from hurt, harm, and danger.

Trust in the Lord with all your heart, And lean not on your own understanding. (Proverbs 3:5)

To trust in the Lord means that you have total faith and belief—that unshakeable, unmovable, total confidence in Him. Don't place your trust in mankind, relying on human wisdom and understanding; it only gets you deeper in trouble. **It is better to trust in the Lord than to put confidence in man.**

(Psalm 118:8) In all your ways acknowledge Him, And He shall direct your paths. (Psalm 3:6)

This verse is one of my favorites that I particularly meditate on: the understanding of casting all my cares on God, putting Him first in all things. I acknowledge there is no true success without Him. Obeying His directives of calling on the Lord in all things will guarantee divine direction from God.

In the Old Testament Book of Daniel, chapter three, there is an account of three Hebrew boys named Hananiah, Mishael, and Azariah. King Nebuchadnezzar, King of Babylon, changed their names to Shadrach, Meshach, Abednego. They have a testimony of a **stormy situation** they endured because they trusted and worshipped the only true and living God. They refused to compromise and serve a false god (the king's earthy image). They were thrown into the fiery furnace, and in the midst of the fire was the Son of man *(Jesus)*. His very presence withheld the flames, bringing victory for the faithful committed men of God.

In the Book of *Acts (16:25-31)*, these two soldiers of the Lord had a powerful reaction in the midst of their persecution. Paul and Silas had a **stormy situation**, being beaten and put in prison because they gave a helping hand to a woman who was demonically possessed.

After they had suffered much affliction, they still brought forth an atmosphere of praise and worship unto God, even while being in turmoil, shackled in solitary confinement (prison). The scripture says, "But at midnight their reaction to their storm was duly noted." Let me set up the scenario as I glean through this text: I imagine a place not like the prisons of today. The prison must have been dark, damp, and dreary, with rodents running around. Dirty, unsanitary conditions— their open sores getting infected from the flogging. In this dark moment of these men's lives, they did not complain. They expressed gratitude toward their Lord and Savior! Instead of breaking out of jail, in the physical realm, they broke out in praise and worship unto God. When the praise and worship went up, suddenly, God divinely moved: the earthquake shook the prison's very foundations, and the jail door opened, and the chains came off of them and the other inmates. Having almighty God with you makes the difference in the midst of every storm.

CHAPTER 14

In Pursuit Forward!

T otal confidence in God will cause you to be a disciplined disciple with a faith that is motivated, continuously pressing toward the prize (their goal).

Purpose driven and God-centered. Proceed steadily on the path of righteousness, regardless of the inevitable circumstances of life's heartaches and problems that all humanity will face unequivocally (with no exception). No matter what we go through, we must be assured of this fact: God is strategically working everything out for our good.

Two very important facts: In the pursuit forward!

(1). We must acknowledge, understand, and accept that problems will come.

(2). Action and reaction to the situation: either you will be victorious or suffer defeat. It's your choice: fall apart or trust God *("The Problem Solver").*

Fully Persuaded to Press on!

The Apostle Paul was in pursuit forward! His perseverance and sufficiency was based upon his personal relationship with Christ. He was fully convinced that nothing or no one could ever stop him from obeying God's divine directives. This is seen in the New Testament epistles he was inspired to write. Paul carried out his assignments, for his capability in the press was only in the ability of his creator. We discover through such profound writings that it was not an easy journey at all for Paul nor for Christians. His trust in Jesus—leaning and depending on Him through the hard times, jail times, scourging, and many haters— would be added to his résumé of accomplishments. Through all Paul's hard trials, he pens this verse: **I can do all things through Christ which strengthened me: (Philippians 4:13).**

When the pressure of life comes my way, I continue on praying and praising God for who he is. He has given unto me joy unspeakable and overcoming strength.

(Nehemiah 8:10) **Do not sorrow, for the joy of the Lord is your strength!**

As one who has also endured many hard times in my own life, speaking from a Christian prospective, God never said it would be an easy journey, but he did say he would never leave us nor forsake us. *(Hebrews 13:5)* **for he hath said, I will never leave thee, nor forsake thee.**

His word is a guiding light unto me, helping each of us every day to keep our eyes focused on Jesus and not on circumstances; our dependence rests in God. *("The Lord is my helper"),*

So that we may boldly say, The Lord is my helper, and I will not fear what man shall do unto me. (Hebrew 13:6)

Pressing forward, trusting in the Lord with all my heart, I am constant and consistent in kingdom building and determined to venture on in my life's journey, staying on the path of righteousness. As a representative of the gospel of truth and the good news of Jesus Christ, there is no compromise for having a warrior attitude, knowing that the battle is not mine—it's the Lord's!

For I am persuaded that neither death nor life, nor angels nor principalities nor powers, nor things present nor things to come, nor height nor depth, nor any other created thing, shall be able to separate us from the love of God which is in Christ Jesus our Lord. (Romans 8:38-39)

The Apostle Paul wrote to the church at Philippi, thanking the believers, for they had been a Blessing, providing money to him. At the time of his writing from prison, he was not freaking out because of his circumstances; he had learned to be content through the hard times, and he was in a place of contentment. **Not that I speak in respect of want: for I have learned, in whatsoever state I am, therewith to be content. (Philippians 4:11)**

When I think about this word "press," the dictionary defines it as "steadily applied weight; of application force; exerting pressure." The imagery that comes to mind is an iron—the application process, the smoothing or ironing of clothing—using an electric iron with an adequate amount of heat needed for the task to remove the wrinkles. Sometimes, wrinkles remain, so another process is needed, pressing the steam or mist button or applying a little starch to get that pristine, creased look. When looking at this process of ironing from a spiritual perspective, the form of pressing is like a child of God facing difficult temptation and trials—like hot heat being applied to one's life—like the stubborn wrinkles in garments—but one must remember to apply starch and press the stream or mist button *(daily devotion and prayer)*. Continuously praise and worship God, regardless of circumstances. Activate your faith, which will smooth out the wrinkles and dissipate them in the name of Jesus. **I press toward the mark for the prize of the high calling of God in Christ Jesus. (Philippians 3:14)**

CHAPTER 15

Stay In the Safety Zone!

When I became a parent, it was so important for me as a mother to make sure I did everything that I could to keep my daughter safe. As she grew up, I monitored her carefully while she was outside playing and made sure that I knew who her friends in the neighborhood were. In this society in which we live, there is danger lurking in many forms to bring harm to us or our loved ones.

Protection and safety are of vital importance for humanity. We are protected by police officers and the armed forces. Being unprotected is an uneasy feeling. This can be nerve wracking and even scary at times, but there is a totally different assurance when one has the confidence in God's loving presence.

Be motivated each and every day to keep moving forward and stay focused, being God-centered and purpose-driven. I am grateful for His protection that is renewed daily. I now understand what it is to feel safe in Him, being conscious of not making knee-jerk decisions without consulting God through prayer in Jesus' name. I do this in order to prevent unnecessary mistakes and accidentally falling into sin or letting the trail wear me down.

Therefore, my beloved brethren, be ye steadfast, unmovable, always abounding in the work of the Lord, for as much as ye know that your labor is not in vain in the Lord. (1 Corinthians 15:58) We must stay vigilant in the Lord (guarding yourself by praying), having an eagle eye vision that will allow you to maintain a clear path. The Bible directs believers: **Watch and pray, that ye enter not into temptation: the spirit indeed is willing, but the flesh is weak. (Matthew 26:41)**

Cultivate a relationship with your heavenly father through daily devotion (reading, singing, and praying) and presenting our body as a living sacrifice, holy and acceptable, which is our reasonable service.

(Romans 12:1) **I beseech you therefore, brethren, by the mercies of God, that ye present your bodies a living sacrifice, holy, acceptable unto God, which is your reasonable service.**

Travelers must be vigilant and pay attention to all the signs on the road, watching out for potholes and obeying all warning signs. Travelers are in the ark of safety, carefully observing the road, where life's traffic consists of **"Chaos and Sin,"** which will try to edge or nudge you off this heavenly safety zone. God has provided a safe haven, where angels are encamped all around to protect and keep us for hurt, harm, and danger. **(Psalm 34:7) The angel of the LORD encampeth round about them that fear him, and delivereth them.** *(Crisis HotLine): Support is always available 24/7.* When I am in a spiritual or emotional crisis, *I WILL CALL 777-God-Help Ext: JESUS and try www. CoveredByTheBloodOfJesus.com*

By dialing this safety zone (calling on your heavenly Father) making all of your concerns, prayer, supplication, and your requests known unto God, you are holding nothing back. God is listening attentively to those who belong to him by faith in His Son Jesus. He is our life line (especially for me). Remaining in the pathway of God is key! His word is like a lamp, which is a light that guides my steps. Being steadfast, firmly fixed, and stable, constantly staying on the right course, no matter what comes my way, will allow me to follow in the steps that the Lord has ordained for me. I will not allow anything to hinder my relationship, nor will I self-sabotage the movement of God in my life. Disobedience will definitely place one in the danger zone. When one gets off and finds oneself appeasing their flesh, misrepresenting the Gospel of Jesus Christ, there are consequences for ungodly action—twofold.

(1). No hedge of protection
(2). Worldly rewards

For the wages of sin is death; but the gift of God is eternal life through Jesus Christ our Lord.(Romans 6:23)

Power! Points! Residents of the Safety Zone:

(1). Steadfast and unmovable: Be still and know that He is God!

Being steadfast under the pressures, knowing that I'm not alone, and having endurance in the face of hard trials are essential for the safety zone. I have assurance that a prevention team is always on my side *(The Father, Son, and Holy Spirit)*.

Having a health care provider (Jesus-care) has given me everything I need with pre-existing injuries, so I can continue in the faith and not be moved from the blessed hope of the gospel of Jesus, which is my sustaining keeping power.

I have been in the hospital many times for surgery, having many caregivers. Each time I went In, I would pray to God for those in the medical professions: doctors, nurses, assistants, and last but not least the lab tech who comes to draw my blood. Being in the hospital is a golden opportunity to witness about Jesus, and there were always God moments. Imagine hearing someone who just had a total knee replacement ministering relentlessly from their hospital bed. With my leg strapped in this apparatus that helps the knee bending process, I religiously prayed for people and led them through the sinner's prayer. A few did accept Jesus as their Lord and Savior, glory to God! I learned that I was in the master's hands, because He was my doctor in the sick room.

I didn't let fear or worry over take me.

> *(2).* **Rooted in Jesus Christ:** Is when one's faith grows, as they press into His presence daily.

As ye have therefore received Christ Jesus the Lord, so walk ye in him: Rooted and built up in him, and established in the faith, as ye have been taught, abounding therein with thanksgiving. (Colossians 2:6-7)

Being in the zone is a region set by a special characteristic, where activities are restricted by God. I am determined to stay on this narrow path – no compromising allowed. As I think about this in my mind, I can picture a sign that says *"A life of obedience will keep you safe."* Having confidence in God, activating my faith, and trusting in the only one who has given me this great opportunity of being part of His heavenly family is a wonderful thing. His daily protection keeps us safe from distractions that would normally lead us astray on alternate detours. God's unconditional love and divine care toward His children is eternal.

Hold thou me up, and I shall be safe: and I will have respect unto thy statutes continually. (Psalm 119:117)

The fear of man bringeth a snare: but whoso putteth his trust in the Lord shall be safe. (Proverbs 29:25)

Luke brings us to a time in this text *(Acts 12:5-19)* when the early Christian church was suffering many trials and persecutions continuously. If they were found preaching, teaching, and worshipping in the name of Jesus, they would be arrested and thrown into jail; some even suffered a horrible death. They could not endure such persecutions on their own, becoming prayer warriors and not willing to throw in the towel nor take matters into their own hands, like trying to break Peter out of jail. They were consistently praying to the one and only God that could help them in their time of need. Prayer is the source for all our problems during dire emergencies. Making intercessory prayer was made unto God on behalf of those affected. This was a power-packed prayer meeting, with unity amongst believers together on one accord, praying for their fellow brethren to have deliverance unto the LORD. **Peter therefore was kept in prison: but prayer was made without ceasing of the church unto God for him. (Acts 12:5)**

The effectual fervent prayer of a righteous man avails much. (James 5:16)

Prayer is a dialogue between God and those who are in covenant relationship with Him. By receiving Jesus as their Lord and Savior, only through them does prayer avail much.

Jesus' faithful fellowship *(unity)* in prayer with his Father was continuous throughout his earthly ministry.

And when he had sent the multitudes away, he went up into a mountain apart to pray. (Matthew 14:23)

And in the morning, rising up a great while before day, he went out, and departed into a solitary place, and there prayed. (Mark 1:35)

Christians must be persistent in prayer, for Jesus teaches his disciples about the power of prayer. *(Matthew 6:5)* **And when thou prayest, thou shalt not be as the hypocrites are:** Praying is not using intellectual jargon *("eloquence of words")* while one is speaking words out of their mouth. **But thou, when thou prayest, enter into thy closet, and when thou hast shut thy door, pray to thy Father which is in secret; and thy Father which is in secret; and thy Father which seeth in secret shall reward thee openly. (Matthew 6:6)**

The Lord's Prayer! (Matthew 6:9-13; Luke 11:2-4)

Praise: When one expresses true, sincere prayer that's heartfelt and spirit-led, it is that kind of love, full of gratefulness unto God, which is an attribute evident in a child of God's life. *(Psalm 34:1)* **I will bless the Lord at all times, his praise shall continually be in my mouth.**

Study the Word God: *(2 Timothy 2:15)* **Study to shew thyself approved unto God, a workman that needs not to be ashamed, rightly dividing the word of truth.**

God's word consists of the basic essentials and nutrition that help us to grow mightily into Christ's image. Christians are equipped with the tools they need in order to fill their daily God-ordained assignment, reaching the non-believer successfully.

We must apply ourselves by meditating repeatedly on the Holy Bible *[spiritual food]* for spiritual growth. Study until it comes alive within you, with earnest application of the word. Here is a key point: the scripture will provide and enable a person with the effectiveness to proceed forward. In studying this road map carefully, we will be able to produce fruit in due season.

My brothers and sisters, if we neglect to study the life-changing inspirational Word of God, you will hinder the growth process. It will render you unequipped and unskilled for the war that is going on each and every day of our lives. You must know what arsenal to use and adequately suited-up with spiritual weapons of engagement to be ready at all times. We are on "active duty status" for war as a believer in Christ inevitable, but we must always pursue victory as soldiers who are more than conquerors!

Stay in your own lane!

When I am driving my car, staying in my own lane, one thing I don't like is when someone behind me is tailgating—one who is in such a hurry on the road, seemingly unconcerned about other vehicles or pedestrians crossing the roadway. I just believe that those who speed past me only end up stopping at the red light. "What's up with that?" Bad driving habits can cause catastrophic effects for those who are just trying to make it to their destination safely.

My only daughter has uttered these words to me as a passenger in my car: "Mom, you're driving too slow, and how come you don't switch lanes?" My response to her was that there is no rush; I'd rather be safe than sorry. I have been there, done that, and have the scars to show for it.

Looking at this as an example for a motorist, this is what might take place in an accident. Someone is traveling and speeding excessively, under the influence of alcohol or illicit drugs, and they are not paying attention to the road or other motorists. Being distracted by texting, eating, or mechanical failure, their judgment is impaired, and their reflections are slow. They are unable to realize the seriousness of an accident that could occur. These are some of the things that will cause you to get out of a safety zone. Disregarding the safety of others—a person in this state does not understand the possibilities of fatalities *(innocent lives lost)* for motorists, passengers, and pedestrians. A person who is careless and irresponsible has placed themselves and others in harm's way.

Safety should be the number one priority in everybody's life, because you only have one life to live, so live the life of a Christian, being born again spiritually as a new creation in Christ and no longer traveling out of control by steering the wheels of life on my own. I decided to give up being under the influence of sin, and now I am intoxicated with the Holy Spirit *("New Wine")*. This analogy is given in various scriptures. We can perceive the symbolism of one who is drunk with wine or liquor; they are under the control of alcohol. A Christian who is Spirit-filled *("New Wine")* is governed by the Holy Spirit.

(Acts 2:13) These men are full of new wine. (Ephesians 5:18) And be not drunk with wine, wherein is excess; but be filled with the Spirit.

On this new journey with the LORD, being fully persuaded to remain in his care (safe and secured by his grace and mercy), I am staying in my lane and doing what God has called me to do. I desire = to abide in the presence of God all the days of my life. If you stay in the will of God, he will take out the old life of its sinful pleasures and replace it with the new, born again life.

(Psalm 91:1) He that dwelleth in the secret place of the most High shall abide under the shadow of the almighty.

"Out with the old and in with the new" is a concept of acceptability for all who are willing to follow the instructor *(Holy Spirit)*, who will enable you to have spiritual insight, keeping your eyes on the prize while traveling in the safety zone.

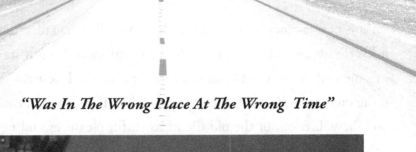

"Was In The Wrong Place At The Wrong Time"

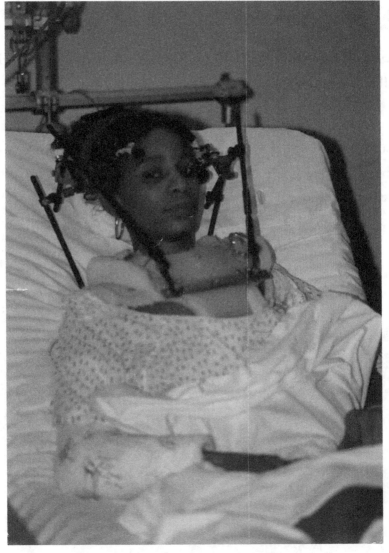

CHAPTER 16

A Purpose-Filled Life!

(Romans 8:2) **And we know that all things work together for good to them that Love God, to them who are the called according to his purpose.**

God has a plan and purpose for all Christians and is quite capable of performing His will. Believers must fully realize this important fact: it is not in our capabilities or powers to do anything apart from His divine will. Through him, in him, and by him, we live, move, and have our being.

(Acts 17:28) **For in him we live, and move, and have our being; as certain also of your own poets have said, For we are also his offspring.**

I can now truly make this affirmative statement: I live with the assurance that everything which has been designed for my life will come to pass. *The dictionary meaning for purpose is the reason for which something is done or created or for which something exists.*

Death had to get out of my way, because God has a plan for my life that is purpose-filled, along with divine assignments. When I think about "divine destiny" *the call of Jeremiah, a young man with a purpose-filled life*, comes to mind.

(Jeremiah 1:5-7) **Before I formed thee in the belly I knew <u>thee</u>; and before thou camest forth out of the womb I sanctified thee, and I ordained thee a prophet unto the nations.**

Then said I, Ah, Lord God! behold, I cannot speak: for I am a child. But the LORD said unto me, Say not, I am a child: for thou shalt go to all that shall send thee, and whatsoever I command thee thou shalt speak.

In the Bible, a young man named Jeremiah was called by God to be a prophet to the nation of Judah. He was commissioned with confronting his own people with a message that proclaimed God's judgment against them for their idolatry.

Their unfaithfulness to almighty God shows that they were a disobedient people in need of correction and discipline. The task that this prophet had was an unpopular one. The message that he was commanded to tell his countrymen wasn't received. Instead of repenting, they persecuted and rejected the word of the Lord given by the prophet. This was a tremendous task placed upon this chosen vessel, but God will not place more on you than you can bear. Despite Jeremiah's many excuses (his inability to articulate, no credentials, and youthfulness), God told Jeremiah what his purpose was and that he would not be alone or speak on his own accord.

The writings of the Prophet Jeremiah have encouraged me to have total reliance on God. I understand that he has chosen me for his own purpose, and he shall perform and complete the work.

And we know that all things work together for good to them that love God, to them who are called according to his purpose. (Romans 8:28)

Knowing your purpose when faced with situations that are sometimes devastating is important. I can recall an alarming report from my doctor, advising me that I needed surgery because of a cyst in my ovary. My husband and I sat in the doctor's office and were told that I was in a grey area, and, to make sure that I did not have ovarian cancer, surgery was needed (There are no grey areas in God). I was told prior to surgery to pack a suitcase, just in case the result came back positive. I stood on my faith in God, still following the doctor's advice—whom God uses in medicine for their knowledge and expertise in that field *(of practicing medicine)*. Engulfed with several trials and tribulations, I was also told by physicians some years ago that the mammogram taken revealed a mass, and I needed a biopsy. I was told that I could have uterine cancer. I thank God all the test results were negative! One thing after another occurred in this traveler's life. Many more trying situations appeared right behind the other. Thinking the storm had blown over, *[but not]*. My menstruations would last for two months straight abnormal bleeding nonstop. This situation in which I experienced, cause me to recall the stories in the Bible. About the woman with an issue of blood for twelve years, who was determined not to let anything or person stop her from getting rid of this issue that plague her life. She spent everything, paying physicians who could not help her at all. *(Luke 8:43)*

The great Physician Jesus was in her view she push pass the flock of people. Her answer for what she was going through was before her, bending low to the ground she touch the border of his garment and immediately her issue of blood stanched. *(Luke 8:44)* Jesus said unto her, daughter, be of good comfort: thy faith hath made thee whole; go in peace. *(Luke 8:48)*

The word of God claimed the storm that was raging in my life as I endured the pain and all that came with this issue of blood. When the blood flow stopped for two months; my doctor then said that I should have a surgical operation (procedure) that would stop the blood flow.

I encourage every believer in Christ to let the peace of God rest in you as you stand strong, for during the storms you will find true peace, and it is awesome to know that you're not alone. I am so grateful for God's abiding presence in my life. He is on my side, and His Holy Word reassures me by letting me know that, through all that I encounter, it will be well. It's not over until He says so. It was not my time to check out. I still had some work to do by preaching and teaching the gospel of Jesus Christ.

AFTER JESUS' RESURRECTION! FOR 40 DAYS! Purpose Fulfilled!

Our Lord and Savior Jesus is the one who provided the only way to Heaven! He made appearances again and again. He presented himself to his disciples. He gave convincing, unmistakable evidence standing before them while being risen back to glory. It was a period of 40 days.

He expounded on things relevant to the kingdom of God *(divine instructions)*.

(Acts 1:3) **To whom also he showed himself alive: after his passion: by many infallible proofs: being seen of them forty days: and speaking of the things pertaining to the kingdom of God:** *On Emmaus Road. (Luke 24: 13-30)* Two men, Cleopas and Simon, were traveling to a village called Emmaus. They were having a conversation amongst themselves about all that had happened concerning Jesus. The two men met Jesus, unbeknown to them, as he stood among them, walking and talking to them. *(Luke 24:15-16)* **And it came to pass, that, while they communed together and reasoned, Jesus himself drew near, and went with them. But them eyes were holden that they should not know him.**

After Jesus spoke with them and expounded on the scriptures, he abided with them until evening with a fellowship meal, in which Jesus took bread, blessed it, broke it, and gave it to them. At this moment, the disciple's eyes were opened; in other words, they gained *"spiritual sight"*, and then they knew who he was. Then, Jesus vanished out of their sight.

Jesus still had finishing touches on his earthly ministry: to impart vital instructions to his disciples before departure. He did not ascend to his father until completion of his divine assignment *(Luke 24:44)* **And he said unto them, these are the words which I spake unto you, while I was yet with you, that all things must be fulfilled, which were written in the law of Moses, and in the prophets, and in the psalms, concerning me.**

Renee E. Woods

As I end, thank you so very much for spending time on this journey through the pages of this God-ordained book. If you still have any doubts that Jesus died and arose from the grave for your sins to reconcile you back unto God, my answer to you is yes! Jesus is the only way in which man can be saved, and there is no other name. It's not in any religion or a denominational group—only a relationship with Jesus. Without Jesus, one is doomed to face eternal damnation. Jesus can and will save you from the very pits of Hell!

I truly implore you to follow these simple instructions: ask God to please open your understanding and to forgive you for unbelief. You must believe in the redemptive work of Jesus. When Jesus made another appearance to his disciples *(Luke 24:36-43)*, they were terrified and frightened. They thought they had seen a ghost. Our Savior put their fears at ease. He proclaimed "Peace be unto you" and gave them proof, showing the marks on His hands, feet, and side.

(Luke 24:39) **Behold my hands and my feet, that it is I myself: handle me, and see; for a spirit hath not flesh and bones, as ye see me have.**

And even after showing them evidence, they still did not believe. *(Luke 24:40-41)* **And when he had thus spoken, he shewed them his hands and his feet. And while they yet believed not for joy, and wondered, he said unto them, Have ye here any meat?**

These believers needed spiritual sight, so Jesus opened their understanding, so they might understand the scriptures *(vs. 45)*. The word of God is your proof; believe and receive!

Align yourself with His word. **(Romans 10:9) That if thou shalt confess with thy mouth the Lord Jesus, and shalt believe in thine heart that God hath raised him from the dead, thou shalt be saved. For with the heart man believeth unto righteousness; and with the mouth confession is made unto salvation.**

So, will you right now ask God, this very moment, to come into your heart, to save you, to fill you with His Precious Holy Spirit? Tell God that you do believe that Jesus came down in the flesh and died (for your sins) and arose. God, who loves you, is merciful, kind, and is waiting for you.

The Divine call! God reassured Jeremiah

(Jeremiah 1:8-10) Be not afraid of their faces: for I am with thee to deliver thee, saith the LORD. Then the LORD put forth his hand and touched my mouth. And the LORD said unto me, Behold, I have put my words in thy mouth See, I have this day set thee over the nations and over the kingdoms, to root out, and pull down, and to destroy, and to throw down, to build, and to plant. When Jeremiah proceeded on his journey to accomplish his assignment, there was no stopping him! This was not because of his own abilities but doing his God-ordained assignment and fulfilling his purpose in the LORD.

Now that I am in my season of manifestation, which consists of a purpose-filled life, I believe that everything God has spoken through the prophets of the Lord over my life shall now be revealed. I am dedicated more now than ever before by submitting myself to the Holy Spirit, who is driving me to receive and achieve all God has for me. I'm in awe of God! The aspect of clarity is in understanding the scriptures and spending quality time in prayer with God. This is the key to being zealously motivated, knowing that our main purpose in life is to please God.

Abiding in the secret place of the almighty is total intimacy and personal, private prayer time.

Being never alone, the comforter *(our personal guide)* is on this journey with us, as we adhere to the instructions that will fulfill the assignment of God. The Holy Spirit, who is the third person of the trinity, is leading and guiding us into all truth. He is the greatest teacher, steering us into position for our journey. Yes, there are troubling times, where we become weary in difficult situations, but His strength is made perfect in our weakness. Trials come to make us better, not bitter; there is a process to regeneration and sanctification, which builds spiritual maturity.

There is a plethora of scriptures in the Bible that encourage us to keep on keeping on, with blessed assurance that our change will come. **And let us not be weary in well doing: for in due season we shall reap, if we faint not. (Galatians 6:9)**

I'm proceeding on with the joy of the Lord. My weary days and emptiness of this world's disappointments weigh me down no more. Trials come and go, turning into triumphs. I am victorious in Jesus with a determination to make a difference in the lives of others as a living testimony of a traveler whose life is transformed forever.

Changed by the resurrection power of the blood of Jesus, my steps are now ordered on the pathway of heavenly direction. **The steps of a good man are ordered by the LORD: and he delights in his way. (Psalms 37:23)**

The designer, who is God, has arranged my steps for his purpose and plan for His glory and honor. He made me a representative, following the systematic pattern of Jesus' footsteps as I travel along the way, having prepared me for this journey with the confidence of knowing He is always with me. So, I put one foot in front of the other, walking in a forward formation as a warrior on the battlefield, marching in the direction of the call of God for my life.

One day, the Spirit of the Lord said to me, "I brought you back from death for a reason and a purpose: preach my words." This is the mission to reach those who need the truth of the Gospel of Jesus. **He brought me up also out of an horrible pit, out of the miry clay, and set my feet upon a rock, and established my goings. (Psalm 40:2)**

To all the haters who don't believe that women are to preach the gospel or teach, shame on you! Jesus made the way—not man or any religious denomination or organization.

No one can stop what God has ordained—those for whom His son bled, died, and arose from the grave. Be they male female or a little child, the Creator is the head of orchestrating the life of all mankind. **There is neither Jew nor Greek, there is neither bond nor free, there is neither male nor female: for ye are all one in Christ Jesus. (Galatians 3:28)**

I dare not intentionally disobey God! Woe unto me if I preach not the gospel of Christ, for he is my way maker; he alone saved me from a burning Hell. By God's goodness, which leads to repentance through faith, I've escaped judgment with no condemnation, and all charges were dropped. It's only because of the Love, Grace, and Mercy of almighty God.

He has keeping power, so just go ahead and walk in obedience and pursue your divinely-appointed assignment from your Heavenly Father. Just say, "Yes, Lord, here am I. Use me. I will obey." Believers must fight the devil, instead of fighting one another. Church, it's truly self-examination time. Check yourself by going before God in prayer and asking Him, "Am I wrong about certain scriptures?" I say to you, my sisters and brothers, there is only one Holy Spirit, and we should all, as believers, be of one accord. Don't become a hedge blocker, for somebody will stumble. Potholes and traps will be placed in the way of the traveler, with all kinds of divisions and wrong signs to block the roads. *(Proverbs 4:12)* **When you walk, your steps will not be hindered.**

It's your time! Design purposes!

To everything there is a season, and a time for every purpose under heaven. (Ecclesiastes 3:1) King Solomon, the writer of the book of Ecclesiastes, penned these very prolific words in **verse 3:1**, speaking about everything having its time and seasons for one's purpose in the life of a believer. All events are orchestrated by God; everything transitions at an appropriate time, and change is essential. A divine purpose and plan was designed especially for you; it's very important for one to know and understand the manifestation and promise of God for kingdom assignments.

In the book of Esther, we learn about a story of an appointed time and assignment of a Jewish woman, named Esther, who was under the care of her cousin, Mordecai.

And he brought up Hadassah, that is Esther, his uncle's daughter: for she had neither father nor mother, and the maid was fair and beautiful; whom Mordecai, when her father and mother were dead, took for his own daughter. (Esther 2:7)

When God has a purpose and plan for your life, he doesn't lay it out for one to fully understand.

Esther became Queen of Persia and was used by God (**"Design purpose"**).

Queen Esther was informed by Mordecai about the fate of all the Jewish people. The massacre was plotted by the king's chief minister, Haman. God uses ordinary people. Mordecai told Esther what needs to be done, and if she holds her peace, another person will be raised up. **(Esther 4:14)**

Esther went to her husband, the King, aware that she could be put to death. She went anyway; her purpose was completed: saving the Jewish people.

We have to walk in obedience and do whatever our heavenly father has called us to do; it's your destiny fulfill it in Jesus' name.

God's design, purposes, and plan were for His Son to make a way out of no way for humanity. Jesus paid it all. Please, receive His pathway and join His royal family to enter into everlasting life. Jesus told his disciples after opening their understanding: **And said unto them, thus it is written, and thus it was necessary for Christ to Suffer, and to rise from the dead the third day:**

And repentance and remission of sins should be preached in his name among all nations, beginning at Jerusalem. (Luke 24:46-47)

Jesus' ministry was fulfilled; the work of redemption was accomplished and completed. Your question has been answered. *"Yes, Jesus is the only way to heaven."* Don't miss out.

ABOUT THE AUTHOR

Renee E. Woods is a charismatic motivational speaker, who is the author of, Yes Jesus is the only way! She is an ordained Pastor, Evangelist, Teacher and Preacher of the Gospel of Jesus Christ. Pastor Woods is a graduate who received a Doctorate of Divinity Degree. She has completed several Academic Courses, and attain Certificates of Completion. "Mental Health Case Management, Substance Abuse counsellor, Youth Mental Health aide and a first responder. An Entrepreneur in her own right, she is a Empowerment coach of Renee's Inner Beauty. She and her husband Robert are in Ministry together. Renee and Robert are the parents of one daughter and three granddaughters and reside in Hillsborough county Florida.

Printed in the United States
By Bookmasters